Super S

Superhero Therapy for Facing Disaster-Related Trauma

Also by Janina Scarlet

Super Survivors:

Superhero Therapy for Facing Disaster-Related Trauma

Janina Scarlet, Ph.D.

We don't always choose our call to action
but we can choose how we respond to it.
This is your call to your heroic journey.
Will you answer it?

ROBINSON

ROBINSON

First published in Great Britain in 2021 by Robinson

1 3 5 7 9 10 8 6 4 2

Important Note
This book is not intended as a substitute for medical advice or treatment.
Any person with a condition requiring medical attention should
consult a qualified medical practitioner or suitable therapist.

A CIP catalogue record for this book
is available from the British Library.

ISBN: 978-1-47214-586-4

Typeset in Gentium by Initial Typesetting Services, Edinburgh
Printed and bound in Great Britain by Clays Ltd, Elcograf S.p.A.

Papers used by Robinson are from well-managed forests
and other responsible sources.

Robinson
An imprint of
Little, Brown Book Group
Carmelite House
50 Victoria Embankment
London EC4Y 0DZ

An Hachette UK Company
www.hachette.co.uk

www.littlebrown.co.uk

To all the doctors, nurses, firefighters, first responders, volunteers, grocers, farmers, and each and every one of you who helps to make this world a better place

Contents

Chapter 1
The Origin Story

She texted me in the middle of the night, her message urgent: 'This virus. When it comes to you, you need to know what we didn't know here in Italy. I wish someone had told me. I am telling you now, so that you have a better chance than we did. People are dying. Stay inside! Wear a mask when you're going out. This is serious. This is life or death.'

My friend's warning still rings in my mind, millions of people having been diagnosed with the coronavirus, hundreds of thousands dead as a result of it. Initially, it had seemed like something out of a faraway dream or a movie, something that wasn't real, something that could not happen here.

And then it came.

I was under strict instructions from my doctor to practise physical distancing and take very careful precautions because of the status of my health. Reading story after story of people who were dying alone in hospitals, away from their loved ones, broke my heart. Seeing the world wrapped up in excruciating pain felt as if my own heart was being wrung out inside of my chest. I saw people who had always been incredibly resilient suffer more than they ever thought possible. I saw people overwhelmed by grief and loneliness, having lost their loved ones and having lost the ability to receive social support.

And at the same time, I noticed something else – I noticed universal kindness and people using their skills, their abilities, their platforms, or any talents that they had, to help those around them. I saw doctors, nurses, pharmacists, therapists and other healthcare providers working tirelessly to help people in need. I saw farmers, truckers and grocers ensure that people had the supplies they needed to survive. I saw people volunteering, often risking their own lives and health to help complete strangers.

Any major disaster can make us feel alone, especially when we have to physically distance from other people, such as during the COVID-19 pandemic. People that survive major disasters, such as COVID-19, Hurricane Maria, the Sri Lanka Tsunami, the earthquakes in Haiti and Japan, as well as numerous worldwide floods, fires, cyclones and heatwaves, can benefit from the ability to find emotional and physical support from others who have been through something similar. In addition, people who have witnessed or survived a violent trauma also can benefit from being able to find support groups in which they are able to share and process their experiences in a safe and supportive way. Unfortunately, emotional support is not always available to survivors of traumatic events, in which case managing the devastating effects of trauma can become an isolating and lonely experience. Worse, because of the tremendous impact of national or global disasters on other people, many individuals who have either lost loved ones or undergone other excruciating events might suddenly find themselves without much-needed support, right at the time when that support is most crucial. It is therefore not surprising that the rates of mental health disorders are spiking in numerous countries, as well as physical health conditions and suffering around the world.

During the COVID-19 pandemic, people around the world have been reporting loneliness, hopelessness and grief due not only to the unpredictability of the health-related and political events, but also due to the loss of their previous coping strategies, such as being able to spend time with friends, going to a pub, café, theatre or a concert, attending sporting events or comic conventions and being able to travel. What's more, this is an ongoing issue, with people continuing to struggle with loneliness, as many have trouble asking for the support that they need to heal and recover.

Most of us have not been taught how to ask for support when we are struggling. In fact, many people have even been shamed for experiencing a trauma reaction or for expressing their emotions. For example, one of my previous clients, 'Lauren' (this is not her real name), has been experiencing depression since she was just five years old. At just five years old, Lauren was subjected to bullying and racist taunts. Her parents worked long hours to support the family and Lauren spent most of her time either in daycare, where kids openly expressed the view that they didn't want to be around her, or with babysitters who were too busy to interact with her. Her parents were exhausted at the end of the day and would go to bed shortly after dinner. As a result, Lauren felt utterly alone.

When she was nine years old, she finally plucked up the courage to tell her mother that she was feeling depressed. At this, her mother laughed. 'Depressed? What do you possibly have to be depressed about?' As Lauren tried to explain to her mother that she felt lonely, her mother shamed her further, stating that Lauren had a house, toys, as well as both of her parents and also her grandparents, whom Lauren saw once a month. Her mother said that other people 'have it a lot worse' than her, as if having material possessions or living relatives must equate to happiness. At this, Lauren was left to believe that her feelings were inadequate, irrelevant and unimportant. In mirroring her mother's indifference towards her own suffering, Lauren also sided against herself, becoming her own biggest critic, and punishing herself for feeling bad.

Three years later, at just twelve years old, Lauren attempted suicide. Although adults often dismiss the risks of child suicide, the youngest case of completed suicide is five years old (in the United States). Thankfully, in Lauren's case, she was revived and was later able to receive the support and care that she required. Specifically, Lauren needed to find a way to process her experience of being racially bullied, as well as the emotional neglect and invalidation she had been through. Invalidation coupled with the damaging effects of trauma can cause severe mental health damage for trauma survivors. Oftentimes, even the most well-meaning parent might come across as invalidating and dismissive if they are unable to grasp fully the extent of their child's emotional and/or physical pain.

Because trauma can be incredibly isolating, this book serves as a way to bring trauma survivors together. To assist you on this journey of healing, you will meet other trauma survivors who have also been affected by multiple traumatic experiences, such as natural disasters, the pandemic and losses of loved ones. Their names and interactions might be fictional, but their stories are real. They will serve as your friends, as your sidekicks, and as your support group.

Through this book, you will be invited to learn and practise multiple skills. Some of these might be helpful and others might feel overwhelming or even triggering at times. Please, listen to your body. It is OK to put an exercise on hold if you are feeling overwhelmed. It is OK not to complete all the exercises and it is OK not to like or implement some of the exercises you will come across. Everyone has different needs and some exercises will suit you more than others. Trust yourself. You are the expert on your own journey. No one else is. Take from this book only what applies to you and give yourself the permission to ignore what does not work for you.

Please take your time and allow yourself to take as many breaks going through this book and these exercises as you need. This is your safe space, your sanctuary. Here, you are welcome and accepted exactly as you are and in any way you need to be.

Every person and every superhero has an origin story and for some people and some superheroes that origin story might begin with a traumatic event. An origin story is the initial event, which might have tilted our life in a different direction. For example, Bruce Wayne witnessing the loss of his parents in childhood leads to him later deciding to become Batman – the hero of Gotham City – to ensure that no one else loses their loved ones the way he did.

Fig. 1: Zoom session.

An origin story is essentially the very beginning, the jumping-off point, of our heroic quest. My own origin story began after a major disaster as well – the Chernobyl nuclear power plant disaster. I was just a few months shy of my third birthday when the radiation explosion incapacitated me and many others who lived in the region. I spent a lot of my childhood in and out of hospitals, and to this day struggle with numerous health issues related to it. One of the biggest side effects that I experience is that whenever the weather changes, I struggle with severe migraines, which occasionally lead to seizures.

As challenging as some of my physical health issues have been, I have also spent a large portion of my life struggling with the psychological aftermath of this event. It took me more than two decades to be able to say the word 'Chernobyl' without being overwhelmingly triggered by it. And it took even longer for me to fully realise the impact of this trauma on my mental health.

I was twelve years old when my family and I emigrated to the United States. In school I was the 'weird girl' who did not speak English, did not understand American culture, and came from a radioactive country. Classmates used to tease me, asking me if I glowed in the dark, if I was contagious or radioactive. On most days I just wanted to die.

The bullying was hard enough, but what made my experience especially challenging was feeling excruciatingly lonely. I wanted so badly to fit in, to find a sense of belonging, but no matter which groups I tried to join, I always felt that I was somehow 'a freak' or 'an outsider'. Worse, whenever the weather changed, especially before it would rain or snow, my migraines would spike, making it impossible for me to partake in school or social activities, often leading to further isolation and exclusion by classmates due to me being 'unreliable'.

My entire life changed a few years later, when I saw the first *X-Men* movie. Watching it, I learned about mutants – fictional superheroes, all of whom had a genetic mutation, which endowed them with certain abilities. All of them had been bullied or ostracised because of their genetic mutation and some of them had been exposed to radiation. Just like me. One of the mutants, Storm, even had the ability to change the weather and used her abilities to help other people.

I was stunned. My entire life, I had thought of myself as a victim. But in watching this film, for the first time in my life I thought of myself as a survivor. Instead of being controlled by the weather, I rethought my ability to predict the weather as my superpower.

As I looked around the movie theatre that night, I saw other people who seemed to be as entranced by the film as I was, and I realised that there was a good chance that they too felt connected to the characters. I realised that most people do not learn to understand and process their emotional experiences when growing up and therefore might feel alone when they are in most dire need of support and companionship. I realised that although sometimes our suffering can alienate us, the very fact that we all experience these challenges makes them universal, and I also realised that we can use stories as a kind of bridge to be able to communicate what we are going through.

I came out of that movie theatre excited and inspired and I signed up for my first ever psychology class to study human emotions. Throughout my life, I have come to realise that every person, real or fictional, has an origin story. And for many people, their origin story begins with a trauma. And although we all have an origin story of our own, our origin stories don't have to define us. Origin stories are just the beginning of everyone's heroic journey. The rest of the path is up to you. We might not choose the call to adventure, however terrifying that path might be, but we can choose how we answer that call.

Oftentimes, we might feel overwhelmed or unable to move forward when we go through something traumatic, such as a natural disaster or losing a loved one. In order to help you grow with this experience, you and the other heroes in your group will support one another in working through your origin stories, as well as building paths for your healing and growth.

The following exercise determines your origin story in order to assist you to find your own heroic path and to arm you with the tools and sidekicks that you'll need to fulfil your quest.

Please take as much time as you need with this exercise. You can start and stop if you need to. If you are feeling over-whelmed, it is perfectly OK for you to take a break. You can always come back to the exercise at another time. Listen to your body and please feel free to give yourself the permission to do what is right for you.

Origin Story Exercise

Many people go through numerous losses, excruciating physi-cal or emotional pain, and feelings of loneliness and alienation. Just like our favourite superheroes or real-life heroes, we too have an origin story. An origin story can be a memory of a terrible tragedy, an accident or a moment when we decided to make different choices. Take a few moments to consider your own origin story. Do you remember a defining moment that shaped you?

It could be a traumatic moment, such as an assault, witness-ing or surviving a disaster, or a loss of a loved one. Sometimes, an origin story could be a happy event, such as starting a new job, having a child or moving to a new city, all of which might be exciting but can also sometimes cause extreme stress and anxiety in some cases.

Or perhaps it was a 'death by a thousand cuts' – numerous experiences of bullying, child abuse, abandonment or other experiences, which at the time felt unbearable?

For some people, there are multiple origin stories, perhaps multiple experiences that have affected them in multiple ways. If this is your experience, then please choose the most recent origin story for this exercise, one that brought you here, one that took your life in another direction and one that has possibly caused you undue stress and heartache.

If you are willing, please write down your origin story in a few sentences or a paragraph in regard to what happened to you and how it affected you. You can write it below or on a sheet of paper. Please don't worry about grammar, punctuation or your handwriting for this exercise. Alternatively, you could draw your origin story as one or more comic book panels. Regardless of how you decide to participate in your origin story, remember that it is for your eyes only and no one else needs to see it, unless you want them to. Give yourself permission to be as honest as you need to be, knowing that you can always shred the page if you want to. And if writing down your origin story feels unsafe for any reason, feel free to silently reflect on your origin story instead.

_____
_____
_____
_____
_____
_____
_____
_____
_____
_____

Thank you for participating in this exercise in any way you were able. This process is not easy, and it takes courage to revisit the trauma of your past. It takes just as much courage to be able to set boundaries for yourself or others when you need to step away from this work and to honour your body and your feelings. Whatever you need to do today is exactly the right step to take.

You are not alone in your experiences. Your fellow group members are here with you and for you. I am going to invite them to share their experiences if they so choose.

Erika is the first to volunteer. 'I can share. I'm a doctor. I would guess that my origin story would have to be the COVID-19 pandemic. I first became aware of the coronavirus in March 2020, when people started coming into the clinic where I worked. They were sick, sicker than they'd ever been, and antibiotics weren't helping them. My patients had pneumonia and were reporting chest pain. I tried sending them to the hospital, but they were turned away.

'The protocols that were in place at that time were only for people who had travelled to Asia and had a fever. There were no protocols for people who did not meet these criteria. My patients were scared and suffering. I had one patient who kept coming back to see me because his antibiotics were not helping him; he was getting worse and worse. I felt like I was doing something wrong. When you are in primary care, people trust you; they keep coming back to you. I felt like I didn't know what I was up against. I finally gave my patient an antiviral cocktail, which saved his life. No one else would treat him. They were just turning him away.

'I would see patients from early morning until eight or nine at night and then stay up till midnight or later reading up the latest research articles about which medical protocols were best. I would get so furious with some of my colleagues for giving their patients drugs that lowered their immune system while they had COVID-19 symptoms, and not giving them antivirals. Often their patients would come to see me after the other treatments had failed. I often felt helpless and incredibly guilty for not having all the answers. I would just research every moment I had, scouring the latest data to see how I could help.

'I gave my patients my personal number just to make sure they could reach me in an emergency. I'd be getting calls at three in the morning and would barely get any sleep.

'And then I was also pulled to work in the hospital, in addition to my clinic work. The hospital said that they needed as many doctors to help with patients with COVID as possible. I was exposed several times and, thankfully, tested negative.

I was working nearly a hundred hours per week, sometimes more, especially with research, notes and follow-up care.

'I was so anxious that I would bring COVID home to my kids that I would change in the garage and run into the house to shower, scrubbing over and over before I could hug my husband or my kids. What little sleep I got would be interrupted by calls or texts from my patients, or from numerous nightmares and panic attacks I started having.

'I would cry all the time. My patients were often frustrated with me if I couldn't get back to them the moment they called, my family barely saw me, and because my husband and I are both doctors, our friends and neighbours completely abandoned us. We became the neighbourhood pariahs. People would cross the street just to avoid us and people would be afraid to be near us in the grocery store, where we often had to go because we were running out of detergent from washing our scrubs and lab coats every day. People would only call if they needed medical advice, forgetting that I'm a person. Sometimes I forgot that part too. Sure, to the media, we were seen as heroes – people applauding us as we were walking into work, cheering for us at 7 p.m. on a nightly basis. But to the people we knew, to our friends and neighbours, we were something to be feared and avoided. And . . . it's just . . . it's been very hard is all.' Erika sniffles through the tears.

'I wish I could give you a hug right now,' Liz says. 'Meeting virtually like this is not easy, especially since it has been my life for so long now. I'm a nurse and I'm used to being in the hospital, in the ER. I'm used to working with patients.

Fig. 2: Exhausted-looking Erika.

'I tend to hold the hand of my patients if they let me because I find that it eases their fears and suffering. There's something so comforting about that, it has always been my favourite part of my job.

'I have two autoimmune conditions and also take immune-suppressing medications, so I was ordered to stay home and just see patients virtually.

'Like Erika, I felt really helpless and overwhelmed. The protocols were unclear and were changing every day and I was terrified of doing something wrong. Because of the uncertainty of this virus, it was unclear what patients should do, what their safest bet would be. Because of the fear of COVID, patients would often refuse to go to the hospital; people who really needed to go.

'I had a patient with a recent kidney transplant who contracted an infection and needed to go to the emergency room. She was refusing to go. It made sense. Poor thing, she said that if she got COVID, she wouldn't survive for sure. I spent four hours researching to find the safest hospital for her to go to and two more hours pleading with her to go.

'But what I feel every day more than anything is guilt. My colleagues are out there, saving lives, and I'm working from home. I have felt isolated and alone. You know those 7 p.m. cheers that Erika mentioned? Those aren't for me. Those are for them – for the ones who are out there saving lives. Me . . . I . . . don't know.

'I also feel so very alone. I feel sad. And I feel guilty for feeling this way. I keep telling myself that I should be grateful, you know, that I'm safe and I don't have the right to be sad. Other people have it much worse. Two of my co-workers died from COVID, more got sick, most lost at least one family member, some lost more than one. Me, I feel like I lost myself.

'It's been months since I've touched anyone. Since I've held anyone's hand.

'I remember after 9/11, a group of us got together and we just held each other. Same thing happened after Hurricane Katrina hit. I flew over there to volunteer and at the end of our shifts as we would be exhausted and burned out, we just held one another and cried. And there was something so healing about that. It was because of both of these events that I decided to go into healthcare.

'But being far away from everyone, not being able to grieve with the people I know, not being able to hug the people that I love, that feels like death sometimes. And I just . . . I just want to be able to hug someone again.'

Hazeem speaks next. 'Thank you so much for sharing this, my friends. I wasn't sure what to write for my origin story. I think the Kashmir earthquake is my origin story in many ways. My uncle and his family all died in the earthquake. It was very sudden. It was the first time I realised how quickly the people you love could be taken from you. And then the COVID pandemic came. Both of these have changed the way I am interacting with my family, with other people, and with myself. They have changed everything.

'I run a grocery store and see people every single day. But it is not the same as it was before. I used to talk to everyone who came in but now, they just rush out. One of my employees takes care of his wife who has cancer, so I told him to just stay home to avoid any potential exposure to her. I pay him what I can, but I don't ask him to come in. My other employee started having symptoms and tested positive for COVID-19. He and his family are recovering now. I got tested as well and thankfully tested negative. I used to go to my brother's house to see him and his family once a week, but I don't go any more to make sure that I do not get them sick, in case I've been exposed. My brother and his wife had a baby four months ago and I still have not met my nephew.

'My father died from COVID six months ago and my brother and I had to say goodbye to him over video. I was half a kilometre away but I could not see him. I could not hold his hand. I could not hug him when he died. I lost five more people after he died; one friend and four acquaintances all died within a four-month interval. None of them were able to have anyone by their side, and none of them had a memorial service. It doesn't seem right.

'It's strange. I see people every day at my store, but I feel more alone than I have ever felt in my life. I find myself worrying that I might have done something wrong. I wipe all surfaces non-stop and I fear that I might make a mistake, and someone will get sick and die because of something I did or did not do. Like Dr Erika, I have nightmares, I feel inadequate and frightened. I have started to pull away from other people, but it is not in my nature. I do not recognise myself any more. I don't know who I am any more. I don't remember the reason for waking up in the mornings, other than because I have been doing it for many years and because my customers need their groceries. I no longer find joy in my work. I no longer find joy in my life. I am scared of some of the thoughts I have when I am alone. I do not know what I can do to feel better. I am losing hope every day.'

'I feel you, Hazeem,' Shawn says. 'Feeling alone even around other people and wiping surfaces all day long, I can definitely relate to that. I guess my origin story began on 9/11. That morning, when I learned about the attacks, I pedalled all the way to the Brooklyn Bridge on my bicycle and I saw the towers fall. I felt so helpless. I wanted to scream. I wanted to help. I couldn't do either.

'This event shook me up so much that I decided to become a firefighter. I never wanted to feel that helpless again. Fighting fires, saving lives, spending time with my family, it was my life. Was.

'Now, I feel just as helpless as I did back then. Because our calls became restricted to fires only, our once busy schedule became much less demanding, leaving me with hours upon hours in the day to just think about the pandemic. I isolated myself from others as much as I could at work to ensure that I didn't expose anyone in case I was sick, and to ensure that I didn't expose myself and bring the virus home to my wife and kids.

'I first learned about the pandemic back in January of 2020, but it was in March when my family and I returned from our vacation that it felt like we'd come back into a dystopian film. The streets of New York were empty. Quiet. Eerie.

'When I went back to work, it felt like a ghost town. The city that never sleeps looked more like one overrun by a zombie apocalypse. The only sounds you could hear were the sirens.

'I went from spending my days with my work crew to spending most of them alone at the fire station, wiping everything, washing my hands dozens of times, and reading everything I could about COVID. Sometimes, if I had to work a twenty-four-hour shift, I would spend that entire time cleaning. I am so anxious that I can't sleep, so I just stay up and try to distract myself until I pass out from exhaustion. I'm having nightmares, I'm losing sleep, and losing friends. And I keep thinking that I shouldn't even be complaining. Other people have it much worse. I don't know.' He sighs.

'I can relate to that feeling,' Celeste says. 'I feel guilty all the time, too. I am an accountant. I work from home. I have a loving wife and a wonderful dog. I don't actually know anyone who died. But I can't help how anxious I feel. I've become obsessive to the point that I not only wipe every surface in the house, but I ask my wife to do the same. She says she's sick of playing into my anxiety.

'I haven't been able to leave the house in months. Just the thought of it gives me a panic attack. And when I have panic attacks, I have trouble breathing and I wonder if I have COVID. I keep checking my temperature, I keep researching my symptoms and I keep calling my doctor. I feel incredibly guilty because I wonder if I am preventing other people from seeing my doctor when I schedule a call with him.

'I just feel stuck. This anxiety feels like a double-edged

sword. If I try to ignore it, it grows like dragon fire and after a while I feel like I'm suffocating from panic. If I give in to anxiety and do all the checks and all the cleaning, I don't have relief either, because my mind will ultimately find something else to be anxious about. My wife and I are fighting more than we ever have and it's all because of my anxiety.

'I feel like a prisoner, not just in my own house but in my own mind. And there's no escape. I don't know what else to do at this point.'

For a moment, no one else is speaking. And I just want to take a few seconds to breathe with all of you. Perhaps taking a moment to build some safety into this experience, to notice that right now, in this very moment, you are right here, and that right now, in this very moment, you are safe.

It is completely normal and understandable that you would feel exactly how you are feeling right now. Whether your feelings are of anxiety, devastation, anger or even numbness, all of your emotions are perfectly OK and perfectly allowed. Most people would feel the same way you do if they were in your situation during this time.

Just the mere *feelings* of anxiety, depression, anger, panic and grief do not themselves constitute a mental health disorder. Instead, our symptoms can become a disorder when they get in the way of our regular functioning, such as by preventing us from going to work or school or from attending to our regular responsibilities. For example, someone might have feelings of anxiety on a regular basis and if these emotions are preventing them from leaving the house or attending to their expected responsibilities, and are affecting their desired level of function, then we would say that this person has an anxiety disorder. The good news about anxiety disorders, as well as depression, post-traumatic stress disorder (PTSD) and many other disorders, is that they are treatable. In this case, the word *treatable* does not mean that after the treatment we would no longer have these feelings. Instead, it means that you might learn ways to better manage these feelings and to follow your own heroic journey even if you encounter some of these obstacles along the way.

Some people think that people can only develop PTSD through combat experiences. However, PTSD can also occur if someone has a near-death experience, such as surviving a car accident or being a victim of a violent crime, or witnessing a tragedy, such as 9/11. Similarly, people can develop PTSD if they have gone through abuse, assault, prejudice, bullying, as well as an unexpected loss, including the death of a loved one, a traumatic break-up, or the loss of a home. Finally, many people do not realise that they might also develop PTSD if they go through a life-threatening illness, such as cancer or COVID-19.

Whether you have experienced COVID-19 yourself, know someone who has, or were otherwise affected by an illness or a tragedy, you are allowed to feel the way that you feel. Whatever your experiences are, this journey is your own and that means that you are the expert in what you need and what works or does not work for you. Please give yourself the permission to make this journey your own in every way possible. Participate as much or as little as you feel safe and comfortable doing and give yourself the permission to take frequent breaks. You do not owe anyone a report or an explanation about your progress. It is perfectly OK for you to do this your way and in your own time.

Just like Batman and Wonder Woman, you too have an origin story and, just like some of your favourite characters, you too are a superhero; this is your own path to your heroic journey. Your acceptance letter is below:

Dear superhero,

Welcome to the Super Survivors Academy. You have no doubt already experienced a lot of pain and trauma and borne the feelings that you never thought were possible. But you are a survivor. You are already a superhero and your mission is not over. You change the world for the better on a regular basis and have already helped countless people. You might not realise this, but there are people alive today because of you. And your work is just beginning. You have a journey of healing and heroism ahead of you.

Thank you for being wonderful. Please keep superheroing and don't forget your cape.

Chapter 2
Monsters and Obstacles

Everyone experiences trauma differently. Some feel the effects of trauma right away, some feel nothing and seem to be 'fine' for a while. Sometimes, the effects of trauma can resurface months – or even years – later. For some, the effects of trauma can feel like a sudden flashback, for others they can be a panic attack, whereas for others still they can present as depression or irritability, and wanting to be away from people.

When faced with a disaster or a tragedy, it is completely normal not to feel normal because the very world we live in might no longer make sense. It's understandable that we might feel angry or overwhelmed by grief and anxiety. For most, the world we believed to be safe no longer feels like a safe place, and that's bound to make anyone anxious.

Many people experience a sense of shock or disbelief at the start. That is partially because events like 9/11, Hurricane Katrina or the global pandemic might be too much for our minds to emotionally process at the start. We might under-estimate the impact of these events on our mental health either because we have been taught to suppress our emotional struggles or because we might not know how to process such terrifying events overall.

'I can definitely relate to that,' Liz says. 'In my family, we were taught never to show our weakness, to just smile even if we are hurting, and to always make the best of every situation. When my nana died, we were only allowed to cry at the funeral. After that, we were not allowed to be sad or look sad. So, even when I felt sad, I would force myself to smile because that was what was expected of me. But the truth was that I often felt like I was wearing some kind of a mask, you know?

'Whether kids were teasing me in the playground, whether people wouldn't promote me – stating that there were budget cuts but then promoting my white colleagues – whether it was a death in the family, I would just pretend like none of it bothered me. But each event would tear another piece from my heart to the point that now it feels like there is a hole there that nothing else can fill.'

'And if I may ask,' I say, 'what does that hole in your heart feel like?'

Liz thinks about it. 'I guess . . . it feels like there's something pressing on my heart, but it feels empty at the same time. It's weird. I also have this knot in my throat that feels like I am suffocating and also like I want to scream.'

I place my hand on my heart, feeling her pain. 'It's very brave of you to share that, Liz, thank you. Sometimes we feel that sensation in our throat either when we have unprocessed grief or when we have been suppressing our voice.'

Liz exhales and stares for a moment. 'I never . . . I never cried when my baby brother was . . . he was . . . he died. He was killed in a school shooting. I . . . just focused on my mama. I focused on being there for her. But I didn't realise until just now that I never cried,' she gulps, tears running down her face. 'I . . . this is hard.' She sniffles through the tears. 'I'm sorry, I'm OK. Sorry about that.'

I assure her that she has nothing to apologise for. It's interesting how sometimes we might be taught to suppress, avoid and apologise for the very natural healing strategies that we have had since birth, such as crying, asking for help and taking time to heal. Most non-human mammals take time to hide out when they have been injured; they wait until they have recovered before they go out again. However, due to the social pressures that many of us experience, we do not allow ourselves the same kinds of natural healing processes that our bodies and our hearts need when faced with emotional and physical trauma.

'I get that grieving is important,' Erika says, 'but I don't have time to be having panic attacks in the middle of the night or while I'm at work. I have sick patients to take care of; patients who are dying. And I also have a husband and two kids to go home to, and two parents to take care of. I just need these . . . *monsters* to go away. I need to be able to function without having these feelings slow me down.'

'Exactly,' Liz agrees. 'That's how I feel, too. I don't have time for this. I get nearly a thousand emails per day sometimes, and dozens of messages and phone calls in addition to the patients I see virtually. I don't have time for these emotions. But when they come, it's like a volcano. Whenever I actually allow myself to cry, I have no energy and no motivation for hours afterward, but I still have to keep going. My patients can't be put on hold just because I am falling apart.'

It makes sense, of course, that we might not be able to put our lives on hold, and it seems that disaster tends to strike at the most inconvenient of times, often when we are least prepared for it and have the least availability to greet it at the door. So then, how do we cope with it?

First, let's take some time to identify some of the monsters that you have been facing of late, especially those related to your origin story. Some common emotions experienced after a tragedy or a disaster include:

• Anger	• Hopelessness
• Anxiety	• Impatience
• Depression	• Irritability
• Frustration	• Loneliness
• Grief	• Overwhelmed
• Guilt	• Panic
• Helplessness	• Shame

Which ones have you been experiencing?

'Well, looking at them written out like that, I would have to say all of them,' Celeste says.

'Me too,' Erika agrees.

'I guess for me it's been mostly feeling anxious about doing something wrong, feeling sad for the people who died and the people who are suffering, and feeling helpless, wishing I could do more,' Shawn says.

'Loneliness is a big one for me,' Liz says, 'but honestly, of all of these, guilt and helplessness are the biggest ones. I just feel like I can't breathe sometimes from how overwhelmed I feel, but I feel guilty for feeling this way when I am working from home and others are out there in the front lines, literally saving lives.'

'You are saving lives too,' Erika tells her. 'And by taking on as many Telemedicine appointments as you do, that frees up other healthcare providers to see patients in person. We are all a team and we are all in this together.'

'I appreciate that,' Liz says. 'I just wish I could do more.'

A lot of times we might shame ourselves for not 'doing more', not realising that actually in that moment we are already doing a lot, not realising that our bodies and our minds are already working in triple time on healing and recovering, which is a full-time job of its own. Oftentimes, we might fail to notice how many monsters we have already faced that day. Some people just get up in the morning and go to work. Others have to fight a whole bunch of dragons to get there. Dragons are any challenges that we might face, such as struggling to get out of bed, feeling tired, feeling anxious, sad or lonely, facing a trauma, healing from the loss of a loved one, a job or a relationship, having to interact with people you don't like, or having to do things you don't want to do. Each one of these challenges is a dragon.

Imagine that you are fighting off two or maybe even three or four dragons at the same time with one hand, while trying to do your work with the other. It would make sense then that it would not be as challenging for you to complete your work if you were not facing a group of dragons while engaging in another task. The sad truth is that we often discount the insurmountable effort that it takes to get out of bed when we are faced with dragons on a regular basis.

Fig. 3: Hazeem fighting dragons.

So, let's take a moment to count your dragons. How many dragons have you already faced today?

'Wow,' Hazeem says. 'I did not realise this. I have already faced fourteen dragons today. It's no wonder I feel so tired.' He chuckles.

Typically, when such painful and uncomfortable dragon-like feelings come up, we might feel the urge to run away from them. However, when we do not attend to our emotions, they can intensify in the long term. For example, suppressed or unprocessed grief can lead to depression and panic attacks.

Listed below are some examples of initially painful emotions and what can happen if they are not addressed:

Initial emotion	Emotion resulting from suppression
Grief/sadness	Depression; panic; anger
Anxiety/fear	Panic; phobia; irritability
Loneliness/sadness	Depression; irritability
Self-doubt; embarrassment	Shame; depression
Annoyance; frustration	Anger; rage

What are some of the examples of situations in which you experienced these emotions?

_____

_____

_____

_____

_____

_____

_____

In the same way as for the emotions listed above, if we do not process our traumatic experiences or losses, they can turn into mental health disorders, including PTSD, obsessive-compulsive disorder (OCD), major depressive disorder (MDD) and complicated grief.[1] Anytime we try to suppress anything, we can intensify it. Think of it as shaking a fizzy-drink bottle. If you keep shaking it without letting out any of the pressure, eventually the bottle might explode. Our emotions work the same way.

Here is another example:

The Pink Unicorn Exercise

Close your eyes and imagine a pink unicorn – a fully pink unicorn with a pink horn on top of its head. Can you visualise it?

Now, keeping your eyes closed, I'm going to ask you to completely erase that pink unicorn from your mind and memory for the next thirty seconds. So, do not picture the pink unicorn, do not even think of the words 'pink' or 'unicorn' at all.

Ready? Go.

After thirty seconds, please open your eyes.

What was this experience like?

_____

_____

_____

1 Morina, 2011.

Now, close your eyes again, and this time please focus ONLY on the pink unicorn in your mind. Think only of the pink unicorn, do not take your mind off it for the next thirty seconds, don't think of anything else, and whatever you do, do not get distracted.

Ready? Go.

After thirty seconds, please open your eyes.

What was this experience like?

_____

_____

_____

Hazeem is the first to share. 'It was amusing. I actually laughed during this process. No matter how hard I tried to stop myself from thinking of the pink unicorn, he would appear anyway.'

'Me too,' Erika says. 'I kept trying really hard not to think of it, but it kept popping into my mind.'

Our monsters are kind of like that annoying song that gets stuck in our mind, playing on repeat over and over again at the most inopportune times. The more we try to suppress or push away our thoughts, feelings or memories, the louder and more pronounced they become. But what happens when we purposely pay attention to them?

'It's interesting, when I first tried to focus on the pink unicorn, its image was clearer in my mind,' Erika says. 'But after a while, I had a hard time focusing on it. The image was fading in and out and I was getting distracted by other thoughts.'

'I hear what you are saying,' Liz says. 'You're saying that we shouldn't try to ignore our thoughts and feelings, perhaps focus on them instead. But I don't have time to stop and pay attention to all the thoughts and memories that I go through during the day. And in fact, when I do, it feels like a tidal wave that soaks me from head to toe and is now drowning me and suffocating me. I start remembering things I haven't thought about in years. I am reliving my worst moments. I'm remembering things I don't want to remember. I don't have time to feel this way! My patients need me. I just want to be able to be there for them like I always was before this pandemic ever started.'

'That tidal wave you mentioned, I can definitely relate to that feeling,' Celeste says. 'That's how I feel when I try to leave the house. Or when my wife leaves the house. Or when we get packages delivered. It feels like my house is underwater and is full of sharks that I know are there, but no one can see, and I'm just waiting for them to attack. It's hard to tell what is safe and what is dangerous, so everything just feels dangerous. And despite the fact that I am always wiping all the surfaces, all the doorknobs, and washing my hands until they crack and bleed, I still don't feel safe. I'm anxious all the time, and if I address one of my fears, another one just takes its place. So, in following this pink unicorn example, no matter how much I try to force the unicorn to leave me alone, it just won't leave.'

'I experienced something similar,' Shawn says. 'I just want to make sure that I do the right thing. At work, I want to keep my co-workers safe, you know? They have family members who have risk factors. So, I keep away from them. At home, I want to make sure that I am keeping my family safe. Like you, Celeste, I am scrubbing all the time. It seems the right thing to do but I also realise that it's not sustainable. Stopping feels worse because if I'm not scrubbing, I am thinking of what can go wrong, or what I might have done wrong, and the terror of that possibility is so intense that I start scrubbing again. It becomes like a cat-and-mouse game with my anxiety. My wife and friends try to support me, but they have so much going on already, I don't want to bother anyone, so I just keep to myself.'

As human beings, we naturally want to keep ourselves and our loved ones safe. And so, when we perceive any kind of a threat to ourselves or our loved ones, we react to try to prevent the terrible event from happening. For example, we might jump out of the way of a speeding car or pull a loved one out of harm's way when seeing that car swerving in their direction. This kind of a response is beneficial and helps to keep us alive.

However, when we are exposed to a traumatic event, or, as is the case for many people, a series of traumatic events, including witnessing or learning about acts of terrorism, natural disasters or the global pandemic, or our own histories of abuse, rejection, assault or an excruciating loss, these can all compound to make our nervous system react to otherwise neutral cues as if they are dangerous.[2] For example, a combat veteran or a survivor of a mass shooting might drop to the ground when hearing fireworks, whereas previously fireworks might have been a neutral or even a joyful event.

2 Resick & Schnicke, 1992.

Although many people might experience traumatic events in their lifetime, not everyone exposed to trauma develops PTSD or an anxiety disorder, such as OCD or illness anxiety disorder. It is natural for people who go through something traumatic to be affected by this event. However, when the symptoms begin to interfere with the person's daily function and activities, such as their work, home life and social life, their symptom clusters could potentially suggest that this individual might have one or more clinical diagnoses, such as PTSD, OCD or another (in order to be formally diagnosed, the individual would need to see a mental health professional).

Why do some people develop mental health disorders, while some recover naturally over time? Some people erroneously believe that if our mindset is 'strong enough', we should have neither negative symptoms nor negative emotions. However, in reality anyone can experience a mental health disorder, just as anyone, no matter how 'strong' they are, might at some point have a broken bone, a headache or a cold. People who have family members with mental health struggles are in some cases more likely to also experience a mental health issue, although not necessarily in the same way. Similarly, people who have a history of abuse or trauma in childhood are more likely to develop PTSD, substance abuse or another mental health disorder in adulthood, especially when exposed to another traumatising event.[3]

Although there are many reasons why people might develop PTSD or anxiety, there are some common reasons why these

3 Felitti, et al., 1998.

disorders might linger. When responding to a threat, we understandably want to do everything possible to feel safe again. However, sometimes our very reaction to the perceived threat can prolong our traumatic experience. Specifically, if we react to every cue as if it is dangerous, we don't have the opportunity to learn which situations are truly dangerous and which are safe. So, whether it means washing everything until our skin breaks, avoiding all social contact or avoiding anything that feels uncomfortable, we do not allow ourselves the opportunity to find safety and relief. In fact, by avoiding facing our fears, we are likely to prolong our symptoms and distress.[4]

PTSD, OCD and illness anxiety disorder can form because of how we think and how we respond to our thoughts, feelings and memories. Thoughts are any interpretations we make about the past, present or future events in our life: 'This event occurred because of me', 'The world is a dangerous place' or 'If I get close to someone, I am going to get hurt, so I should keep to myself'. These are all examples of thoughts. Feelings, on the other hand, are typically one-word emotions, such as feeling *sad, angry, frustrated, devastated, ashamed, guilty, helpless, hopeless, lonely, happy, excited, confused* or *overwhelmed*; or physiological sensations, such as *feeling out of breath, light-headed, nauseated, tingly, tense, numb,* or *having a headache* or *rapid heartbeat.*

Both thoughts and feelings can directly affect one another. For example, if you are feeling anxious, you might have more anxiety-related thoughts, such as: 'This situation is unsafe.'

4 Shenk, et al., 2012.

Similarly, if you are thinking that a particular situation is unsafe, you are more likely to experience a spike in anxiety. Furthermore, thoughts and feelings can also affect our behaviours. Our behaviours are any actions that we take (such as cleaning) or avoid taking (such as cancelling plans with our loved ones).

After an exposure to a life-changing disaster, our thoughts, feelings and behaviours might change drastically. For example, you might be waking up with a headache, feeling tense, stressed and overwhelmed. You might be thinking about all the terrible things that can occur, believing yourself not to be able to handle them. And in a well-meaning effort to keep yourself or your loved ones safe, you might engage in certain behaviours, such as over cleaning, over washing, avoiding social situations or creating certain rules for yourself, such as 'so long as I wipe this cabinet three times, my loved ones will be safe'.

'Oh my gosh, I do that!' Celeste says. 'I keep saying to myself, "If I don't wear my socks in a particular order, then my wife and I will get sick." Or, "If I don't use two pairs of gloves instead of one, then one of us will die."'

It makes sense that we want to do everything possible to keep ourselves and our loved ones safe. And sometimes the very methods we utilise to do that might go too far, or even backfire. And often we might understandably feel frustrated and angry that things aren't the same as they used to be. We might not slow down enough to allow ourselves to fully take in the gravity of the situation, often expecting that we *should* feel normal in an abnormal situation. Hence, running away from our symptoms might become our way of life, perpetually waiting to live until we die. In other words, we might not allow ourselves to experience joy in life or move forward *until this goes away*, meaning until our symptoms go away. But as we wait for our symptoms to remit, we might be missing out on import-ant and meaningful life moments through distraction, using substances or social media to numb our feelings, or through avoiding meaningful activities, such as social connections with loved ones.

'You know, I didn't use to be this way,' Erika says. 'Before the pandemic, my family and I would go on vacations, my husband and I had date nights, and I saw my friends. Don't get me wrong, I always worked a lot and had my first baby while in medical school, so I was always used to hard work. But since the onset of the pandemic in 2020, I haven't allowed myself to slow down at all. I keep saying to myself that I'll rest when this is over, but I always find another reason to keep working. I forget the last time I got more than four hours of sleep. I keep wanting to ask for time off but there never seems to be a good time to do the things you want to do. I guess it's hard to find the balance between doing what you're supposed to and taking care of yourself.'

In order to make ourselves safe in an unsafe situation (or a situation we perceive to be unsafe) we might form certain reac-tions, which can include fight, flight, freeze or fawn.[5] In all of these responses, our body might perceive the current situation as dangerous even if it is not actually unsafe. In order to keep us

5 Thompson, et al., 2014; Price, 2013; Walker, 2013.

safe, our body might produce certain chemicals, such as adrenalin and cortisol, which are the body's stress hormones. These chemicals are responsible for preparing our body for survival. Specifically, when our adrenalin is activated, we might breathe faster and our heart might pound so much that we feel the blood pulse in our throat. We might also have dilated pupils, or feel light-headed or on edge. We might have a stomach ache, feel nauseated or lose our appetite. Our arms and legs might feel numb or tingly and sometimes we might feel as if things around us are not real, as if we are in a dream state.

As uncomfortable as these sensations might be, they are not dangerous and, in fact, they can actually be helpful when we are in danger. The rapidly beating heart is allowing more blood circulation to our vital organs, enabling us to think and react faster than we normally would. The accelerated heartbeat can allow us to get the oxygen we need during the potential danger while enabling us to remain active in the situation. Our arms and legs might feel cold, numb or tingly because the blood flows away from our extremities and towards our vital organs to keep us safe. Our stomach might not feel well because if we need to fight for our lives, our body focuses on only the most vital processes, shutting down the less urgent ones, such as digestion. We might feel light-headed and as if things are not real because, in that moment, our mind might work faster than the speed of other events in our environment. Hence, none of these sensations are actually dangerous. In fact, they are in place to keep us safe. In a way, these sensations are the activation of our inner superpowers.

For many of us, we might have felt these sensations when we previously felt unsafe; hence, we might associate such physiological experiences with danger. This means that if something reminds us of a dangerous situation – a loud noise, for example – we might naturally startle and our own startle response might then frighten us further because we might associate those sensations with danger, even though they are not actually dangerous. This means that sometimes we might become afraid of our own fear response.

Although most trauma triggers can activate our adrenalin system (*sympathetic nervous system*), the way that we respond to them might differ. As we already mentioned, people have a variety of trauma responses, including fight, flight, freeze, fawn, and also a combination of these.[6] People who typically react to feeling triggered or threatened through a *fight response* might react in an aggressive or confrontational manner. They might sometimes use absolute control in order to maintain connections, friendships and relationships, and rage and threaten others when they feel emotionally or physically unsafe. They might rage and threaten others as a way of keeping people close, but often end up losing relationships as a result. Sometimes, these losses might further reinforce the controlling behaviours as a way of coping with the perpetuating loss and heartbreak, and as an attempt to keep future relationships from ending. Individuals with this trauma reaction are more likely to be characterised as 'bullies' and might be reacting out of fear,

6 Price, 2013; Walker, 2013.

intentionally or unintentionally hurting others because they also experience hurt in that moment.[7] *Hurt people hurt people*, as the popular saying goes.

According to trauma specialist Pete Walker, the *flight response* happens when people manage their trauma by diving into achievement and work. A person with this trauma response type might become perfectionistic; they sometimes might end up being diagnosed (or misdiagnosed) with OCD when their actions might actually be a trauma response. When people with this response feel triggered, they try to control their work. By perfecting their work or home environment, or by engaging in compulsive rituals, people with this response type are trying to keep themselves safe physically and emotionally. Perfectionism and achievement might also become coping tools to maintain relationships, but in many cases, these very safety behaviours, that were intended to keep the relationship safe, might actually backfire, just as they do with the fight response.

The third type of trauma response, the *freeze response*, can happen when a person is so overwhelmed by the threat they are facing (for example, facing a bear or an abusive parent) that they cannot move or find a way to respond to the given situation. Over time, this response might seep into other areas, such as avoiding confrontation, avoiding serious conversations, avoiding meeting friends, avoiding responsibility and avoiding communication. Individuals with this type of trauma response might feel so overwhelmed when they are faced with any kind

7 Walker, 2013.

of a potentially unpleasant situation that they avoid it altogether. They might fixate over doing things so perfectly that they end up not doing anything at all. In conflicts with loved ones, a person with this type of trauma response is likely not to say anything at all or to walk away, often causing their loved ones to think that they don't care about them. Just like the fight and flight responses, the freeze response is intended to make the person feel safe and reduce conflict, but it often backfires, leading to further conflicts, causing the individual with this response type to further retreat.

The most recently identified type of trauma response is called the *fawn response*,[8] which refers to people-pleasing. People with this response type are likely to give up their own views, identities and wishes in order to appease others. It is not uncommon for people with this trauma response type to have had narcissistic or otherwise abusive parents or partners. It is likely that their opinions were previously criticised by others and they might not have been allowed to express a difference of opinion. As a result, people with this trauma response might be over-accommodating towards others to the extent that they might lose their own voice. They might struggle with setting boundaries, sometimes not realising that they have the right to set them, or the right to say 'no'. They might go out of their way to flatter and boost the ego of others and to make others feel supported and comfortable. In addition, when someone is angry with them, an individual with the fawn response is likely

8 Price, 2013; Walker, 2013.

to grovel in order to keep the peace, apologising for things that they are not responsible for. And much like the other three response types, the fawn response is intended to keep the individual safe but ends up putting them in danger by preventing the individual from setting boundaries and causing them to struggle with advocating for themselves.

'Huh,' Liz says. 'That's interesting, because I can actually relate to both flight and fawn. Ever since I can remember, I was always very hard-working and perfectionistic. I put everyone else's needs above my own. But I also seem to do everything I can to please others. It didn't occur to me until now that I don't ever set boundaries with my workplace and no matter what I am going through, I always agree to help others.'

'I can relate to the boundaries struggle too,' Erika says. 'It's always been hard for me to say "no" to anyone, and now I am barely sleeping and barely surviving. I don't actually think I can keep this up.'

'I have always been taught that you have to be kind to everyone else,' Hazeem says. 'So, it is hard for me to be any different. I am not sure if this is my trauma reaction or my way of life, but I have always been this way.'

Hazeem makes a great point, of course. Helping others is a wonderful core value and one we should all engage in. However, when we are helping others not because we truly want to do so but because we think that we *should*, it might not be functional. For example, if you are pushing yourself beyond your limits, leading to burnout, or physical or emotional pain or suffering, this might not be a healthy response. Sometimes, we might feel obligated to help others just because they asked us for help, often forgetting that we have the right to say 'no' or to let them know that we are unable to help them at this specific time or in the precise way they wanted, but we can help them in other ways.

By learning about our own trauma patterns, by identifying our monsters, which might have become obstacles in our lives or on our journey, we can subsequently make changes to better fit our goals. This week, if possible, see if you can take some time to observe your own reactions to stressful, anxiety-provoking or uncomfortable events and fill out the diary overleaf. If you do not feel safe or comfortable filling it out for any reason, feel free to write your observations on a separate sheet of paper, in your phone, or make a mental observation. Take as much time as you need with this exercise, it is OK to start and stop whenever you need to. Give yourself the permission to do as much or as little as you need to in order to keep yourself safe.

Super Survivors

Situation	Thoughts	Feelings	Behaviours
Friend asked me to help her this weekend	'If I say no, she will be angry with me'	Anxious, nervous, light-headed	Agree to help even though I'm exhausted

Chapter 3
Accepting Your Hero's Journey

A hero's journey begins with a struggle. It's true – every hero faces a difficult choice, a tragedy or a frightening path away from the safety of the status quo at the start of their journey. And most also find healing and meaning along their path.

However, each path might be laden with dragons and uncomfortable choice points, many of them seemingly impossible to overcome, and yet possible in the end. What makes these journeys especially challenging are what some psychologists call an *emotional flashback*.[1] An emotional flashback is what Liz previously described as a 'tidal wave'. It refers to an intense and overwhelming feeling of danger throughout our entire body. It is a physiological memory of a traumatic event that we experience as if it is happening in this very moment. Unlike a *memory flashback*, an emotional flashback does not necessarily occur in conjunction with a memory of the past event, but the physical sensations we might experience in our body could be the same or similar to those we felt when the traumatic event occurred. For example, if you were frequently yelled at by your father when you were a small child, you might sometimes have a memory flashback to that event. On the other hand, you might

1 Walker, 2013.

notice that when your boss critiques you at work, you might feel tense, overwhelmed, deeply ashamed and small. In the latter case, this could be an example of an emotional flashback. In some situations, it is possible to have both a memory flashback and an emotional flashback occurring at the same time.

'Can emotional flashbacks happen because of hurtful family interactions?' Celeste asks.

'Of course,' I tell her. 'Emotional and physical abuse can absolutely affect how we feel both physically and emotionally. Sometimes, years of abuse can be stored in our body and can show up as panic attacks or chronic pain (such as migraines and stomach aches), as well as chronic illness and muscle tension. Sometimes anxiety, panic attacks and physical pain are a manifestation of the pent-up grief or trauma we went through in the past. And in fact, abuse we might have gone through in childhood can make us more susceptible to anxiety and trauma in adulthood.'

'Huh,' Celeste says. 'I never thought about it before; or at least I never put it together before. My mother was always very critical of me. No matter what I did, she would always find some kind of a fault with the way I did my homework or my chores, and I would be punished. But my brother could do no wrong. In my family, boys are valued but girls are not. Boys' education is important but girls are expected to just support the boys. Both my parents would always praise my brother and tell me to be more like him.

'I tried my whole life to make them proud of me, but it was never enough. I graduated second in my class but because I wasn't the first, it wasn't even mentioned or celebrated. But any time my brother got an A on an exam, his tests would be put up on the refrigerator for months.

'I remember I ran into the kitchen where the three of them were sitting one evening and shouted that I had got into Oxford with a full scholarship. My mom chastised me for bragging and then proceeded to tell me how proud she was of my brother for getting an A on his calculus test. My dad then said that it is not very important for girls to go to a university and that I should just get a job and contribute to the family financially. When I refused, there was a big row and my mother slapped me. It was one of the many times that she did. She and my dad called me selfish for going to university instead of working. To this day, I jump whenever someone starts talking to me with an exasperated tone or exhales out of frustration. I am always scared of doing something wrong or making a mistake. I didn't realise until now how tense I feel in my body all the time. Is that why people develop OCD and health anxiety? Because of trauma and abuse?'

'Not necessarily,' I tell her. 'For some people, anxiety is a trauma response, even if it surfaces years after the traumatic event. For others, anxiety disorders, such as OCD, health anxiety, panic attacks, social anxiety, generalised anxiety and phobias, might be a genetic factor. People with family members with anxiety are more likely to have anxiety as well. However, just because we *feel* anxious does not mean that our reactions to anxiety will be the same as those of our family members. Whatever the origin, anxiety is essentially a fear of being unsafe, which can lead to certain actions to try to manage that anxiety. These actions can include avoidance behaviours or compulsive checking, and are essentially a way to maintain control over situations that otherwise might feel out of control.'

'It's interesting. I realise that I am an adult and that I am safe, and I am in control of my life, but I just don't feel safe,' Celeste says. 'I feel scared all the time. It's like the world is just too big to make sense sometimes, you know? Going outside feels too big, too unpredictable, too unsafe. Sometimes my own house feels unsafe, too, so I lock myself in my bedroom. And when that feels too big, I hide in the closet or the bathroom just to have a smaller space to feel safe in. I never knew about emotional flashbacks, but I think that's what might be happening in those moments. I think that when I read about the pandemic or another disaster, I feel scared and my body flashes to my trauma. It's strange, but in those moments, I really do feel like a helpless little girl again.'

'Helpless.' Shawn sighs, looking down. 'I can definitely relate to that feeling. Watching the twin towers fall from across the Brooklyn Bridge, wishing I could be there, helping ... Wanting to do something. Anything. I still feel it in my bones today. And that is how I feel when I am at my station. I want to do more. It never feels like enough. I have nightmares of my buddies dying in the fire with me just watching and not having my radio or my equipment. Not being able to help. I never knew there was a term for it, but I guess emotional flashback is what it might be.'

In addition to emotional flashbacks, many of us are subjected to *moral injury*, especially during a crisis. Moral injury refers to a traumatic event in which the individual has either contributed to or was unable to prevent a tragedy, which can violate that individual's morals and expectations of themselves or others.[2] Active-duty service members, veterans and first responders, for example, might struggle from moral injury if they are unable to prevent the death of a friend or an innocent civilian. Similarly, healthcare providers, firefighters, police officers, and other people who are responsible for the safety and the well-being of others might also undergo moral injury if they are unable to participate in helping others to the degree that they would like or if they are unable to save someone.

'Wow,' Liz reflects. 'Now that you say it, it makes sense. Moral injury. That's what I think I felt when I was seeing my co-workers getting sick or losing family members and I had to work from home. I just ... I feel guilty all the time. All I want to do is help and I never feel like I'm doing enough. I am barely sleeping; I'm scheduling patients seven days a week, but I just don't ever feel like I am doing enough. The truth is, no matter what I do, it never feels enough.'

'That pretty much sums it up,' Shawn says. 'I never feel like I'm doing enough. When I was filling out the worksheet with "Situation, Thoughts, Feelings and Behaviours", I noticed that I was having that thought in response to pretty much all of the events of the day. That then made me feel anxious and caused me to continue cleaning or scrubbing.'

Just as trauma reactions develop with an intention to keep us safe (although in some cases, they backfire), moral injury

2 Papazoglou & Chopko, 2017.

occurs because we care about being a good person and helping others. The inverse of our biggest worries points to our
greatest sense of purpose. That means that if you are worried
about making a mistake that might harm someone, if you are
feeling guilty about not being able to contribute more than you
are able to based on your circumstances, then you feel this way
because you truly deeply care about doing the right thing and
helping people. Recognising this process can help to turn our
[sometimes unhelpful] trauma responses into helpful ones.
And it begins with noticing how we feel, what we think and
what we do.

Noticing how we feel, think and act in any given situation
is one of the many ways to practise *mindfulness*. Mindfulness is
a special way to pay attention on purpose to either our inner
thoughts and sensations or our outer environment. Being able
to notice when we feel anxious, being able to identify when
we might be going through an emotional flashback or moral
injury, can help us to realise what we are going through and
determine what tools we need to use to allow ourselves to get
through that moment.

Most people think that mindfulness is a relaxation exercise,
but that is not necessarily the case. Although mindfulness can
be relaxing, it might not feel this way all the time. Essentially,
mindfulness is the willingness to notice what is already happening either in the body or around us. Noticing that we are
feeling overwhelmed, noticing that our heart rate is speeding
up, noticing the sensation of our breath, noticing the sounds in
the room around us, noticing the taste of the morning coffee or

the smell of the shower soap are all examples of mindfulness. Interestingly, mindfulness practices can be helpful with managing PTSD, anxiety and depression, as well as chronic pain, addiction and other disorders.[3]

The very practice of mindfulness is an intentional and courageous choice because most of the time we choose to mindlessly engage in avoidance of our stressors or engage in rituals to reduce how we are feeling. Mindfulness is the opposite of that. Mindfulness means purposely tuning into our internal and external experiences, one bit at a time, as opposed to disengaging or distracting ourselves.

'This is something I've always struggled with,' Celeste says. 'My mind is always spinning. I guess I find myself endlessly scrolling through social media. I put my phone down only to pick it up again a few minutes later, often not even aware that I am doing it. Then I am mad at myself that I wasted another day barely working, not doing anything productive or useful, and not even able to recharge myself. I tried meditating, too, but it doesn't work for me. I'm just not good at it. My mind is always going to something else. I just can't focus or clear my head.'

'I struggle with mindfulness, too,' Erika says. 'It's funny because I always recommend it to my patients. There's so much research on it being beneficial, so I always tell them to practise it, but I don't have time for it myself.'

It is a common misconception that in order to practise mindfulness, you have to empty your mind and be able to sit

3 Boden, et al., 2012; LePera, 2011; McCracken & Vowles, 2014.

perfectly still, thinking of nothing at all. The truth is that our mind is not designed that way. We are always thinking of something. But, if we give our mind a direction, such as to focus on a mathematical problem or to count items of a particular colour in the room, we are more likely to be present and mindful. However, when we don't have something to focus on, our minds naturally scan for danger. Our brains are by default prewired to problem-solve and to look out for our safety. In fact, when we are resting or doing a mindless task, such as scrolling through social media, we activate the Default Mode Network of our brain. The Default Mode Network is responsible for brain functioning while we are at rest. Its job is simple – to keep us safe by looking out for any potential threats. This does also mean that the Default Mode Network considers the millions of possible scenarios that *could* go wrong, however unlikely. The more we try to mindlessly disconnect from our thoughts, the more our Default Mode Network might be scanning for danger, often increasing our anxiety and PTSD symptoms when our mind is wandering or if we are engaging in a mindless task. However, mindfulness has been shown to be helpful with reducing some of these symptoms and improving many people's functioning by helping them to focus on the present moment.[4]

Many people believe that they do not have time to practise mindfulness, and although it can be very beneficial to follow a formal mindfulness practice, such as guided meditation, informal mindfulness practices can be helpful too. For example,

4 King, et al., 2016.

even getting ready in the morning can become a mindfulness activity if you can take a moment to notice yourself brushing your teeth, having your breakfast, walking or driving. Oftentimes, we might find ourselves running behind schedule and leaning forward as we are walking or driving, as if doing so will get us to our location faster. However, rolling your shoulders back, taking a breath and staying present with your walk or your drive is still going to allow you to arrive in the same amount of time but perhaps allow you to feel a tad less stressed and less tense.

'Ha! I do that!' Erika laughs. 'When I am running late, I am leaning forward in my car. I sometimes imagine that I could push my car to go faster while driving it, but of course, I can't go faster than the cars in front of me. Sometimes I notice that I am holding my breath. A lot of times when I get to work, my shoulders feel extremely tense.'

I like to talk about mindfulness as a way of slowing down in order to speed up. When we are simply rushing around our day, we are using up a lot of the body's resources. When we are caught in the cycle of trauma or anxiety, we might not realise that in the present moment, things might actually be fine. We might be so caught in the loop of eternal mind time-travelling to the awful past or the imagined catastrophic future, that we do not appreciate the present moment.

Let's take a moment to do a brief mindfulness practice now. During this practice you will probably notice that your attention shifts to another thought. This is perfectly normal. Everyone's mind wanders. When that happens, simply notice it, and gently bring your attention back to this exercise.

If any part of this exercise feels uncomfortable or triggering, or if any parts of your body are not accessible to you, feel free to skip or ignore that part of the exercise. You should practise as much or as little as you feel comfortable doing. There is no need to push yourself to do anything that you don't want to do.

Mindfulness Exercise

To start, please sit or lie down in a comfortable position. You do not have to maintain the same position the entire duration of this practice. At any time, you can always shift your position to make yourself more comfortable if you need to, especially if you feel any pain or discomfort.

Take a few moments just to bring your attention to your breathing. Notice if you have been breathing or if you were just holding your breath. Take a few mindful breaths. Notice how your body is moving with each inhale and each exhale.

Notice the sensations of your feet as they are making contact with the floor. If the sensation of your feet is not available or possible, please focus on the sensations of your arms or your lips instead.

Take a moment to notice that at this moment, you are right here, you are not late for anything, and you are not in a rush to get anywhere. You are right here in this moment, doing exactly what you should be doing.

And at any time, if you get distracted or overwhelmed, you can silently ask yourself, 'Where are my feet [or arms or lips]?' to gently bring yourself back to the present moment.

Take a few moments to notice any physical sensations that you might be feeling now, such as pain or tension. Take a few moments to breathe. Not trying to make these sensations go away and not forcing them to be stronger than they are. Just noticing these sensations as information.

Now, take a few moments to bring your attention to your emotions. Our emotions are kind of like the weather – they are always changing. Sometimes, we might feel one way and sometimes another way. See if you can take a few moments to simply notice how you are feeling now – just noticing your emotions at this time.

Now, take a few moments to focus on the sounds around you, while allowing yourself to gently breathe as you're doing so.

Now, take a few moments to notice the temperature in this room.

Now, take a few moments to notice if there are any smells you can detect in this environment, while continuing to breathe.

Take another minute to notice the sensations of your hands and feet in this moment. And then, bringing your awareness back to your surroundings, take a few breaths and allow as much time as you need to re-centre and come back into the room.

Hazeem is the first to speak. 'My father used to say to me, "Hazeem, always remember where your feet are." I remember being confused by this as a small child and then growing up to really appreciate his wisdom in adulthood. And as we were practising mindfulness just then, I realised that I was both present and not present too. A part of me was here and a part of me was with him, being a little boy again, having him hold my hand and telling me that everything is OK.' He wipes his eyes with a handkerchief. 'My feet are here but here is also painful because it means realising that I am here, and he is not. And in a strange way, I also felt like a little boy again, too, just a boy lost without his father. I think this might have been that emotional flashback you were talking about. In some ways I felt helpless but mostly, I felt very sad.'

As he speaks, I notice my own heart feeling heavy, feeling Hazeem's loss, my own eyes watering as I see the pain in his. It seems that all of us swallow our sadness at the same time before we continue.

Mindfulness can allow us to notice our emotions, including unprocessed grief, trauma and other types of loss. By slowing down, we can observe our hearts, our minds and our bodies in real time. We might notice the palpitation of our heart when we feel anxious, the lump in our throat when we have a need to cry, the tension in our shoulders when we feel unsafe or frustrated, or the discomfort in our stomach when we feel anxious or disgusted. Rather than rushing throughout our day, rather than running away from our emotions, perhaps we can greet them like an old friend. Perhaps we can put away the urgency to respond to every text message and every email the moment that it comes through and take a breath or two before doing that. Sometimes taking one breath before opening a new email, starting a new task or seeing a new client can allow us to be present with that task or that individual. In addition, slowing down in this way can allow us to preserve more of our energy, far more than going through our whole day without a moment's break can do. And in most cases, if you take a breath before each task, you will still complete it in the same amount of time than if you rush through it.

'I felt a lot of emotions during the mindfulness exercise too,' Celeste says. 'I understand the idea about slowing down, but it is really overwhelming for me to just breathe and sit with my emotions. When I actually allow myself to remember my past – the abuse – I just feel so overwhelmed, I don't think I can handle it, so I just shut down.'

It makes sense that facing our emotions, especially when they are tied to a traumatic event, can feel overwhelming. Like opening that bottle of fizzy drink that has been shaken for a long time: there might be an eruption, but it will not last for ever. However, we can also slowly untwist the fizzy-drink bottle so as to allow some of the pressure to escape. This means that we can slowly practise observing our emotions in our body as another kind of a mindfulness exercise.

As you might recall, our emotions can feel like an enormous monster, chasing us as we are trying to run away to safety. However, there is a trick: the monster feeds on fear and avoidance, meaning that it becomes scarier and more powerful when we run away from it, but smaller and less intimidating when we face it.

And there is another trick: the monster is more powerful when you face all of its parts together. But if you break down each part of the monster, you can be more powerful when you face it.

Let's look at your symptoms. Many people who are struggling with panic attacks, depression or trauma-related feelings might experience some of these symptoms. Tick or circle the ones that apply to you:

- Tightness and tension in the neck and shoulders
- Tightness in the chest
- Feeling out of breath
- Heart pounding
- Sweating
- Shaking
- Feeling light-headed
- Stomach discomfort
- Feeling like things are not real
- Flushed cheeks
- Other _____

Now, let's take the monster parts apart and focus on each separate element of your emotions. To do so, imagine for a few moments that you are taking your dog to a park (even if you don't actually have a dog). When the dog is on the leash, he's probably excited, hyper and can't wait to be let off it. But once you take off the leash, the dog can run around freely to let out some of its energy until it feels calm and settled.

Now, we are going to do a similar exercise with each of these sensations. We are going to start with the least uncomfortable, the least distressing sensation from the ones you picked above. Got one?

OK, now imagine that you can zoom in your attention to only focus on this symptom or sensation. For example, if you

picked 'sweating', focus your entire attention now on just noticing how sweaty you are feeling in this moment.

Great! Now, we are going to imagine that you took this sensation to the dog park and took off the leash. That means that
just for a few minutes, we are going to only focus on this sensation while allowing it to be here, allowing it to be as strong or
as weak as it needs to be.

If you are willing, I'm going to ask you to close your eyes and
focus only on this one sensation and fully allow it to be here, as
if allowing it to run around in the dog park.

Ready?

Go!

How did it go? What did you notice? Was it tolerable just to
focus on this sensation?

Would you be willing to try another one?

See if you can focus on each of these sensations one at a time
for at least one to two minutes.

What did you notice over time?

The more we can let our emotions 'off the leash', one element at a time, the easier it can be for us to face these emotions
over time.

'At first, it was still very overwhelming,' Celeste says. 'I was
shaking, so I chose to focus on that sensation. Initially, I started
shaking more and I thought that either I'm doing the exercise
wrong or I was going to be the one person who was going to
have a different reaction than those of the other people. But the
more I took the leash off of this sensation and allowed myself

to shake, the more it felt like I could breathe. Then I cried. I just kind of let it out. I was still shaky at the end of it, but it felt more settled overall. The other sensations settled a little bit too, but I can still feel them.'

The paradox with emotions is that the more we avoid them, the stronger and more overpowering they become. But the more willing we are to experience them, the less they hold us back. So, can we do the same for thoughts? As it turns out, we can.

Thoughts, just like feelings, magnify the more we try to avoid them. Furthermore, we oftentimes *fuse* with our thoughts. *Cognitive fusion* occurs when we accept our thoughts as facts. For example, if a supervisor asks you to do a presentation at work, you might have a thought, such as, 'I am not good enough. I am going to fail. Everyone will judge me.' If we fuse with these thoughts, we might avoid doing this presentation, believing these thoughts to be factual. However, our thoughts are essentially movies played by our minds. Some might reflect real life, while others might be pure fiction.

In order to reduce cognitive fusion with our thoughts and reduce the impact of our thoughts on our feelings and actions, we can practise *cognitive defusion*. Cognitive defusion is the process of acknowledging our thoughts for what they are – *thoughts*, as opposed to facts. Cognitive defusion can allow us to mindfully notice that we are having a thought but without getting carried away by that thought.[5] For example, when watching a zombie horror film, if you feel as if you are in the movie and have to run

5 Hayes, 2019.

away from the flesh-eating zombies, you are in a sense practising cognitive fusion. However, recognising that you are watching a film on television (or in the movie theatre) is equivalent to practising cognitive defusion. The purpose of this practice is to create some distance and a safe separation between you and your thoughts to give you some breathing room.

For example, do you ever have thoughts like, 'I am not good enough', 'I'm not attractive enough', 'I'm not fit enough' or, 'If people knew the real me, they wouldn't like me very much'? Most people have thoughts like these. They are hurtful or frightening and feel like they are 100 per cent real.

Our nervous system fails to see the distinction between the *actual* threat, such as being mauled by a tiger, and a thought in which we *imagine* being eaten by a tiger. In practising cognitive defusion, we can practise creating some distance between us and our thoughts. For example, when having a thought such as, 'If I don't exercise, I will be unattractive and no one will love me', we can instead remind ourselves, 'This is just another self-image movie. I am having a thought that if I don't exercise, I will be unattractive, and no one will love me.'

We can think of our thoughts as our own internal movie themes, often related to the fears of losing or never obtaining our greatest passions and desires. Some of these themes include social belonging/connection, personal growth and achievement/ability, self-image and personal danger.

See if you can identify some of the common 'movie themes' that might play out in your mind or if you can identify your own personalised themes.

Common 'Movie Themes'

Social Belonging and Connection:

- I will make a mistake, it will be humiliating, and everyone will laugh at me and then reject and abandon me.
- I will lose someone I care about (to death, abandonment or rejection).
- If I try to get close to someone, I will be rejected.
- If people really get to know me, they will reject or abandon me.

Personal Growth, Achievement and Ability:

- If I try this and fail, I will lose something I care about (job, opportunity, status, etc.).
- If I try something/take a chance/try to change, I will fail.

Self-image:

- This part of me is unacceptable and no one can love or accept me until I change this part of myself.
- Until I can change this part of myself, I am not allowed to be happy or to do things that make me happy.

Personal Danger:

- If I trust someone, they will hurt me.
- If I am not in control of this situation, I will not be safe.
- Because I've been hurt before, it means that it is highly likely to happen again.

If you are willing, see if you can practise rewriting some of your common thoughts as a defusion exercise. For example, 'My social belonging story is telling me that if I try to get close to someone, I will be rejected.' Alternatively, you can say, 'My thought is telling me that if I try to get close to someone, I will be rejected' or, 'I'm having that same old thought/movie playing out in my mind that if I try to get close to someone, I will be rejected.'

_____

_____

_____

_____

_____

_____

_____

_____

_____

_____

'This is an interesting exercise,' Hazeem says. 'I did not realise how many of my thoughts are related to social belonging and self-image. I often worry that I will lose someone I care about. This fear only got worse when my father died. I also worry about making a mistake and getting rejected by other people.'

'I worry about that, too,' Erika says. 'I worry about losing my loved ones and making a mistake all the time.'

'Me too,' Liz and Shawn say at the same time.

***

One type of defusion exercise we can practise, especially with those pesky obnoxious and critical thoughts that just won't leave us alone, is the Ridiculous exercise. In this exercise, we can practise imagining that the thoughts originate from a silly and untrustworthy source.

The Ridiculous Exercise

Sometimes, our anxiety can cause our imagination to think of the scariest scenarios, most of which will never come true. Very often, we assume that the scary thought will happen exactly as we imagine it and we assume that it is accurate.

The truth is that we have many scary thoughts throughout the day and many of them are no truer than a silly thought, such as, 'I am a banana.' However, our anxiety makes us *feel* like these scary thoughts are likely to come true.

Fig. 4

The best way to face this kind of fear-inducing anxiety monster is to make it seem ridiculous. For example, it might be a lot less scary if those monsters were wearing a banana suit or another silly outfit while trying to yell their scary messages at you through a megaphone.

Draw your anxiety monster below but make it look ridiculous. If you can, please feel free to add some things that it might say to you as a speech bubble in a comic book.

How did it go?

Erika giggles. 'I totally imagined a giant-sized banana yelling at me through a megaphone, saying that I don't know what I am doing as a doctor. It was still not easy to hear, but imagining a banana saying it made it less threatening.'

'I struggled with this exercise,' Shawn says. 'It was still very hard to think about possibly doing something wrong and causing someone to get sick or die. I . . . I don't know . . .'

These exercises are not easy and what works for some people may not work for others. It is perfectly OK to take some time to practise these exercises and to focus on observing your thoughts and emotions. It is OK to take breaks from your practices and it is OK to go slow. Whenever you are feeling overwhelmed, consider smaller steps and go at your own speed. You can do this, and your entire team is here with you to support you.

Chapter 4
The Armour of Vulnerability

In our previous few training sessions, we observed our dragons: the emotions, thoughts and memories that we often want to avoid. We talked about some of the challenges of these practices, as well as important benefits that they bring. What did you notice in these practices?

'I've been practising noticing my emotions all week,' Liz says. 'I previously was aware of my anxiety, but I didn't realise how much sadness I have been feeling, too. I broke down a few days ago. It feels like someone died. Many someones. The grief makes me want to scream but it's suffocating at the same time. It's been hard to do anything this week. I feel like I'm just going through the motions now. I feel like I've opened the door that's never been opened before. I just want it to stop.'

'I felt the same as you, my friend,' Hazeem says. 'I too have felt a lot of grief and loneliness. And strangely, I have also found myself feeling less patient and more irritable than usual. These emotions are not common for me, so they surprised me. I found myself feeling conflicted – feeling extremely lonely when I was at home and also very much wanting to be alone while I was at work. I do not understand this.'

Many people have been brought up to believe that we have to

control and suppress our emotions. If we have been doing it for too long, then initially the process of opening the door to face them will be a painful one. We might experience the surfacing of emotions that we don't normally feel, such as grief, irritability and impatience. These feelings are often an indication that we have many unprocessed emotions and need some time for healing and self-care. Over time, this process gets easier and like any other pent-up energy, our emotions will eventually settle, but only if we allow them to be present in the first place.

'This past week, I have been thinking about things I have not thought about in years,' Liz says. 'I remembered so many things, most of them very painful, most of them things I don't want to think about. I know that this is probably helpful, but I just don't want to think about these memories. Some are so painful that I started hyperventilating. It's a good thing I'm a nurse, because I know what panic attacks are. I had never had one until this week. I feel shaky and weak, and I don't like it.'

'Me neither,' Celeste says. 'I found myself crying this entire week and I can't understand why. The weird thing is that my anxiety has been lower. I've hardly engaged in any compulsions this week and my wife and I even went for a walk yesterday. It was nice, but I felt exhausted at the end of it. I don't know why I've been crying so much, and I don't know how to stop being so weak.'

The common misconception across multiple regions and cultural practices is that in order to be strong, we must not allow ourselves to be vulnerable, and that being vulnerable equates to being weak.

But what does the word 'vulnerable' really mean? This

word *vulnerate* in translation from Latin means 'to wound' or 'woundable'. The literal definition of this word states that to be *vulnerable* is to be susceptible to either a physical or an emotional attack or harm. This is true. People who are more vulnerable, such as people who are going through a physical or psychological struggle, are more at risk of being harmed if others are not aware or not careful around them.

And so, it seems that being vulnerable does in fact put us at higher risk of being wounded. But does this mean that to be vulnerable is a bad thing, and does it necessarily mean that vulnerability relates to weakness? Well, here, science says 'no'. It seems that vulnerability has two sides to it. On the one hand, it can make us more susceptible to hurt. But on the other hand, it can also open us up to joy, love and connection.

Vulnerability researcher Brené Brown says that 'we cannot selectively numb emotions; when we numb the painful emotions, we also numb the positive emotions'.[1] Emotions are essentially an all-or-none package deal. This means that we cannot choose to turn off our anxiety, our depression, our trauma or our grief without also turning off our ability to experience joy and a sense of belonging. Without sadness, we might not fully know happiness. Without heartbreak, it is hard to appreciate love. And that means that taking that risk – facing our own fears or our own mortality – and taking the chance of doing something you care about, even if it means risking losing it all, is the purest definition of courage.

1 Brown, 2010.

There is nothing more vulnerable than having a child, entering a meaningful relationship or going after your dream. Each of these comes with a big risk of potential heartache, but despite the risks, many of us choose the courageous course of action nonetheless.

I spent many years working with active-duty Marines who had served in Afghanistan and Iraq. Having endured multiple traumatic losses, they would go for trauma therapy, sometimes not by choice. Many would report to me that they had experienced daily threats to their lives, lost countless friends in the war, and on many occasions did not think they would be able to get home to their family alive. However, many would also state that being in therapy and being vulnerable, having to come face to face with their grief and trauma, was the scariest thing they had ever done.

We would then talk about courage. The word courage comes from the French word *coeur*, which means 'heart', and according to Brené Brown, it used to refer to when we 'speak one's mind by telling all one's heart'.[2] The current definition of the word 'courage' is having the ability to do something despite our fears and also finding [inner] strength in the face of pain and grief. This means that the ability to be present with our pain and grief, the ability to be open with our emotions and to be able to confide in others are the most courageous things of which we are capable as human beings. And that means that rather than a weakness, your vulnerability is the foundation of your greatest strength.

2 Brown, 2007.

'It makes sense to me but is also different than what I was taught,' Hazeem says. 'My parents always said that a man has to be "strong" and he must never be vulnerable. I was told that I have to be kind but not let other people see my weaknesses.'

This seems to be the case for a lot of people, especially in gender-stereotyped families, and especially in men or people who were gender assigned as male at birth, who are often taught that vulnerability is a weakness and that people should hide their emotions. In truth, people of all genders are shamed for showing emotions. People who identify as male are likely to be called *weak* or compared to women as an insult, as if being a woman is insulting, and as if having emotions is exclusive to one gender. Women, in turn, are often shamed by being called 'emotional', 'dramatic' or 'crazy' for having perfectly understandable human emotions, including anger, frustration, insecurity or sadness. Furthermore, gender minorities, including non-binary individuals, trans individuals and people of other genders, are further shamed for expressing emotions or speaking out for themselves.

'I can definitely attest to that,' Liz says. 'My whole life, I was told that I need to defeat the stereotype of the "angry Black woman", and because of that, I shouldn't get angry. This is very hard because there is so much injustice in the world. How could I not get angry? I still remember the way my nana died. I remember how she kept going to the doctor about her stomach aches, and the doctor just kept saying that she needed to lose weight. He never ordered any tests for her. She died a year later from colon cancer and until the day that she died, she kept saying that she trusted her doctor.

'I have come to learn how often women's pain gets ignored by doctors, as well as how often overweight people's pain gets ignored by doctors, and how often Black people's pain gets ignored by doctors. And when you have an elderly, overweight Black woman, some doctors might not take her seriously. Do you know that some hospitals still teach medical students that Black people experience pain differently because they claim that their skin is thicker than white people's? My nana didn't die of cancer. She died of negligence. She died from racism. She died from prejudice, from fat phobia and from misogyny. And I elected to go into healthcare to fight stereotypes and to attend to people's needs.'

'I am so sorry about what you went through, Liz,' Erika says. 'I also have seen my fair share of bad doctors, and thankfully some good ones. To this day, I am still fighting for equality and inclusion in my office. Patients and staff alike will often turn to my male colleague for advice, medical or otherwise. When I suggest something, it might get ignored, but when my male colleague suggests the exact same thing, patients will thank him several times despite having previously been sceptical of me when I provided them with the same opinion. It's frustrating because I'm the one that spends hours of my own time reading the latest research papers to stay up to date with medicine and my colleague does not. Yet when I make a suggestion, some patients and staff members might say, "Let's see what *he* thinks about this." It's infuriating, to say the least, and I completely share your frustration and anger. And like you, I was also taught to keep my emotions down and to try being "likeable", especially since I am a woman. It is hard breaking some of these barriers and sometimes I don't even know how to feel any more.'

It is heartbreaking how often we are taught not to express our natural emotions, how often we are taught that we are not allowed to feel angry in situations that are truly infuriating. Anger is a very important and telling emotion. It lets us know when our rights or the rights of others are being violated. Anger is not a passive emotion. Anger pushes us to action, such as standing up for what we believe in and standing against racism, prejudice, ignorance and oppression. And so, in many of these situations, anger is not only the right emotion to feel, it is necessary. When it comes to oppression and prejudice, anger allows us to stay vigilant and to then have the courage to take action in order to stand up for what we believe in.

Emotions, such as anger, sadness and anxiety, also signal to us that we need support, action and connection. And this kind of connection can be restorative and healing. And just as setting boundaries with toxic individuals and not sharing your emotional experiences with people who are invalidating and shaming towards you is helpful, so is social connection and sharing your emotional experiences with a support group.

On the other hand, emotionally isolating yourself from absolutely everyone can actually weaken your immune system and negatively impact your mental health.[3] Sure, taking a few days to be by yourself, to charge your inner battery, can be healing and re-energising, but to cut off everyone from your life

3 Friedmann, et al., 2006.

when you are going through depression, grief or trauma can actually make your symptoms worse. A recent meta-analysis study reviewing the impact of emotional isolation on people's health in over 300,000 patients found that social isolation poses a negative impact on the person's immune system and poses a high mortality risk. In fact, the people who engaged in prolonged emotional isolation were shown to have the same risk factors as individuals who engaged in chronic smoking or regular alcohol abuse.[4]

'Loneliness is the new smoking' runs the tagline of the *Managed Healthcare Executive* magazine, which summarises several findings on the harmful effects of emotional isolation. The article differentiates physical isolation (not being around others) and emotional isolation (i.e., disconnection and loneliness even when we are around other people). It is the latter, the disconnection from others, that can be especially toxic for our physical and mental health.

Specifically, loneliness and emotional disconnection can lead to increased inflammation and immune problems, higher cardiovascular risk factors, higher risk of Alzheimer's disease, and an overall higher risk of premature mortality in older adults. In addition, emotional disconnection and loneliness can lead to increased mental health pathology, including depression, anxiety, assumptions of worthlessness and burdensomeness, and suicidal ideation or attempts.[5] This means that when we spend our entire life building the armour of disconnection, this

4 Friedmann, et al., 2006.
5 Cacioppo, et al., 2009.

very armour, though it might protect us from failures and disappointments, might also be preventing us from experiencing the essence of living.

But perhaps we can learn to cloak ourselves in a new type of armour, the armour of vulnerability. This armour might not always be comfortable, but it might be essential in our survival. Rather than hiding behind the thick walls of avoidance, the armour of vulnerability allows you to be seen by others exactly as you are. It can allow others to know you, to see you, to understand you, and to love you for you. In this case, wearing this armour would mean having the willingness to have connection with ourselves and others, and to feel with our whole heart. It would mean having the willingness to be open about our pains and fears. It would mean acknowledging our fears of death, of losing loved ones, of our own mortality, as well as acknowledging our own grief. It would also mean recognising our own thoughts and fears of not being good enough, of not belonging, of not being loved, of dying alone, of needing help but being too afraid to ask for it.

'If I were to do that,' Shawn says, 'then I suppose that I would be cloaked in the anxiety of not being able to protect others. I see images in my mind of people I love dying because of a mistake I made or because of something I failed to do. And even though, to the best of my knowledge, it has never happened, I seem to live with a pre-emptive guilt of doing something wrong. I used to think that this anxiety kept me focused, but now ... I don't know any more. It seems to have taken over. It seems that there are times that I am so overly vigilant, that I am distracted ... And if we are being open here, I guess that I am scared. I always wanted to be able to help, to do the right thing. And when there is a fire, I know exactly what to do now. But it's the other times, you know? The waiting. That's when my biggest nightmares play out in my mind.'

'I know it's not exactly the same thing, but I get it,' Liz says. 'After 9/11 and after Hurricane Katrina, when I was volunteering, I didn't feel everything that I am feeling now. Don't get me wrong, my heart was breaking for everyone who lost loved ones and their homes. But somehow, being there, being a part of the helping community, made it easier to cope. Now that I am working from home, I just never feel like I am doing enough and I am much more anxious about making a mistake than I've ever been in my entire career as a nurse, than I've ever been in the past. Somehow, just by not being physically there, at the hospital, with my patients and my colleagues, I feel as if I am failing them. I know that I am still helping but it's just not the same, you know?'

Many people do better in an actual emergency than during less urgent situations. I like to refer to this phenomenon as our *warrior instinct*. People with this instinct are always ready for emergencies and hence are especially helpful in dire situations. However, outside of emergencies, people with warrior instinct might be in a constant preparatory stage – preparing for battle. This is not a bad thing, and in some cases it might mean that we need to rethink what this preparatory stage looks like. Perhaps it might look like reviewing safety protocols, and perhaps it might look like reaching out to others to see how they are doing in order to still be a part of the action.

Sometimes, when we are not directly in the location of where the traumatic events are currently happening, we might feel as if we are not helping. However, we might only feel this way because we are feeling the energy of the tragedy without having a place to discharge it. You see, when we are directly involved in assisting with an emergency, all that pent-up grief, anger and horror about the ongoing tragedy gets released into action. However, when we are in a situation in which we learn about the tragedy but are unable to help because of our circumstances, we are likely to feel not only powerless but also guilty and depressed. This is because our every fibre is telling us that we need to help but we might not be able to help in the way we would like.

The same happens when we learn about a tragedy, such as a mass shooting, an earthquake or a terrible political event, which negatively affects the lives of many. If we do not take action, we are likely to feel angry, guilty, helpless, as well as ashamed and stuck. As these continue to occur, we are likely to feel overwhelmed and desensitised to these events, not because we stop caring, but because we might feel so overwhelmed with our perceived inability to help, that we naturally shut down, as a way to preserve our well-being. However, when we take action to help, even if it is not directly in the way we would ideally like, we are likely to feel more empowered while also helping a cause we deeply care about.

The process of learning to stay with our anxieties and fears is not a light-switch kind of practice. This means that it is not as if you turn on the light switch and now you are able to be open and vulnerable with yourself and others. Vulnerability practice is like healthy eating, it is a practice that we can spend our lives cultivating. This practice might look and feel different for each person. In essence, this practice entails being genuine and authentic with yourself and others. It does not mean that we have to tell everyone our every thought and experience, but it does mean asking ourselves, 'What is the most genuine step that I can take to be fully authentic with myself?' Sometimes, the most authentic step is to set a boundary with others, to ask for some alone time, or to rest. At other times, it might be to ask others for support, to share your thoughts, views and feelings with others, or to spend time by yourself and to be open to these experiences.

'My entire life, I was taught not to be a burden to others,' Celeste says. 'I was taught that I have to always be kind and polite, that if I am having a rough day, I still have to say that I am fine when I am asked how I am doing. It's funny, I love cosplay, and when I dress up as a fictional character who is struggling with depression or PTSD, I feel more like myself than when I am around other people in my regular clothes, you know? In my day-to-day life, I feel like I'm always wearing a kind of "I am fine" mask. Over the years, all I've learned to do is hide and, I suppose, it's just been getting worse and worse. The truth is, I don't think I even know how to be genuine with my emotions, especially when I am feeling scared and overwhelmed.'

In practising being genuine with our emotional flashbacks and painful memories, we can take steps to be present with these experiences.

- First, it helps to acknowledge how you are feeling. Take a few moments to observe your experiences, including your thoughts, feelings, sensations and memories. You don't have to push them away, just observe them.

- Name your experience. Just like you practised naming your story related to your thoughts, you can name your overall experience. For example, you can notice, 'I am having a panic attack' or 'I am feeling triggered by my traumatic experience'.

- Notice where in your body you are feeling these sensations. You might notice that you have a tightness in your stomach or a pressure in your chest. You might feel warm, your hands might feel clammy, or your heart might pound fast. You might feel out of breath or feel light-headed.

- Take a few moments to ground yourself to the present moment. You can ask yourself, 'Where are my feet?' (Or perhaps, 'Where are my hands?' or 'Where are my lips?' if the sensation of your feet is not available to you.) Notice this grounding sensation (your feet) and take a few breaths while noticing this sensation.

- Find emotional safety. You can ask yourself, 'In this very moment, am I safe?' In this case, the word 'safe' implies whether or not you are safe from physical danger. Sometimes we might feel unsafe, especially when we are triggered or overwhelmed, but we might actually be safe. If you are not safe, then get to safety immediately. If you are safe, take a moment to notice that. Remind yourself, 'In this very moment, I am safe.'

- Notice what you need in this moment. Do you need some time to breathe? Do you need a break from what you are doing? Do you need a hug? Do you need to cry? Do you need to feel safe again? Just observe your inner needs without any judgement, just noticing what they might be.

- See if you can, at least for a brief moment, comfort yourself the way that you would comfort a small child. Perhaps you might say, 'I know this is scary and uncomfortable right now. You are safe. I love you and we will get through this together.'

- If possible, reach out to a friend or another caring individual that you feel comfortable talking to.

'These seem very helpful, but they are also very challenging,' Celeste says. 'I've never learned anything like this before. It feels foreign, like it's meant for everyone else but not for me. It feels a little strange to offer this to myself. It was nice but strange, too.'

It makes sense that these skills might be challenging if you have never learned them. In fact, most people do not learn how to support themselves when they are going through a difficult time. The truth is that every person in the world suffers at one point or another. Every person in the universe feels alone sometimes. And sadly, the very times that we are alone, when we are in the greatest need of human support and affection, might also be the times that we are most likely to disconnect from others, further hurting ourselves. But what we might sometimes fail to realise is that having the courage to share our own pain with another person might allow them to feel less alone as well. Your very own path through your darkest moment might become someone else's map to healing. And your ability to share your experiences with others can not only help you, it can help your support person as well. When you let someone else know what you are going through, you are making a very profound statement. You are essentially saying, 'I am suffering. And chances are, you might be too. And maybe, just maybe, we don't have to suffer alone.'

'I think I am realising that I wish I could have a friend,' Hazeem says. 'I wish I could let someone else know how alone I have been feeling and be a support system for them, too.'

'I am happy to talk to you anytime, Hazeem,' Liz says.

'Thank you, ma'am. I appreciate that. I would like that very much,' Hazeem says. 'Other than the people I see at the store, it has only been me and my cat, Marshmallow. I do not have anyone else to speak to. So, if you would be happy to sometimes talk virtually, I would enjoy having a friend.'

'Put me down too,' Shawn says.

'Me too,' adds Celeste.

'I would love to join too when I am able,' Erika adds.

Finding support groups, even virtual ones, can allow you to find your own sidekicks, the Robin to your Batman, in a way. Having sidekicks, companions or other support individuals essentially has the inverse effect to loneliness on our physical and mental health.[6] Specifically, people who have meaningful

6 Bellosta-Batalla, et al., 2020; Xu & Roberts, 2010.

social support (even if it is virtual) appear to have significantly better physical and mental health compared to people who do not report having adequate social support. In addition, although stressful and tragic life events, such as job loss, divorce or the death of a loved one, put people at higher risk of premature death, people who have meaningful social support do not appear to share this risk.[7]

One of the reasons that people who are able to be vulnerable with others and have meaningful social connections live longer could be because meaningful connection stimulates the release of certain chemicals in our body, including endorphins, opiates and oxytocin.[8] These chemicals can improve our mood, lower our physical and emotional pain, and allow us to feel a sense of joy and connection, and they can be naturally made in our body when we form a meaningful connection with someone.

Oxytocin, specifically, is a very important chemical when it comes to our healing journey. This substance is made by the hypothalamus, the main hormone regulator of our brain. Oxytocin is both a hormone and a neuropeptide – a kind of molecule used by brain cells (neurons) to communicate with one another.[9] Oxytocin has been shown to be extremely helpful at improving our heart-rate variability and improving our overall heart health,[10] as well as lowering our inflammation, improving our gene expression, and potentially decreasing

7 Xu & Roberts, 2010.
8 Bellosta-Batalla, et al., 2020; Xu & Roberts, 2010.
9 Bellosta-Batalla, et al., 2020.
10 Higa, et al., 2002; Kemp, et al., 2012.

our mortality rates.[11] Furthermore, oxytocin can also help to reduce and prevent PTSD and depression,[12] as well as anxiety[13] and psychosis.[14] Interestingly, although oxytocin typically soothes overall anxiety, it can occasionally increase social anxiety, in particular when it comes to the fear of losing an important social connection, such as a friend or a loved one. It seems that this hormone is involved both in anxiety about losing social connections and in soothing that very anxiety.[15]

I tend to refer to oxytocin as our *inner magic potion* because of its many positive impacts on our health. In some ways, oxytocin is a kind of 'love potion' that can help us to foster meaningful relationships with others, increasing the feelings of trust and connection. And in turn, when we begin to open up to others, this chemical is naturally released into our system, strengthening our bond with the person with whom we are connecting on a deep vulnerable level. This means that oxytocin can help to strengthen our bonds with others and also that our meaningful bonds with others can help to boost the oxytocin levels in our system.[16]

Oxytocin is also involved in establishing a sense of connection with people who have similar hobbies (such as the same fandom, video game or sports interests) and core values, which is why we are more likely to trust people who share our

11 Epel & Lithgow, 2014.
12 Arletti & Bertolini, 1987; Flanagan, et al., 2018; Frijling, 2017.
13 Grillon, et al., 2013.
14 Martins, et al., 2020.
15 Crespi, 2016.
16 Crespi, 2016.

interests. In addition, oxytocin is also an important component in childbirth, sexual activity, breastfeeding and hugging behaviours, which is why physical affection, such as hugs, can become positively reinforcing in relationships. Seeing adorable baby animals and baby humans also releases oxytocin, producing a caring and empathic response in the observer. Oxytocin allows for mentalising (an empathic understanding of how others might feel in a given situation) and the willingness to help, promoting both social and altruistic behaviours. Finally, oxytocin is also released when we are either offering social support to others at a time of distress or receiving support from others during this time.[17]

Taken together, these research findings suggest that in being open and vulnerable with others, we are essentially building up our body's oxytocin levels, which in turn can help to soothe our distress, reduce our depression, anxiety and trauma symptoms, reduce our inflammation, improve our heart health and potentially prolong our lifespan. Thus, it makes sense that it feels like we are dying on the inside if we lose a loved one or go through a social disconnection due to a break-up, a conflict or the global pandemic. The reason why it might feel as if a part of us is dying is because in some sense, it is. The grief of losing our relationships and social contacts is a real type of grief and, just as if barbed wire was pulled through your vital organs, these disconnections can feel excruciating. And it also means that when we can re-establish or create new meaningful

17 Crespi, 2016.

connections with people, even virtually, or perhaps establish a sense of connection within a group, such as a fandom, or form a meaningful heartfelt connection to a fictional character, we might feel less alone. And this connection could potentially supercharge our body's oxytocin levels, almost as a kind of superhero suit, powering us up, activating our inner super-powers, allowing us to function at our highest capacity levels. If so, this means that vulnerability is the most powerful armour you can build to become the strongest version of yourself that you can be.

Fig. 5: Love is oxytocin.

'Medically speaking, it makes sense that being vulnerable and having close connections will boost our oxytocin levels,' Erika says. 'But practically, that is very hard for me. I'm originally from Peru and my culture and my family value kindness, especially kindness to others. I was taught to be kind to everyone else but self-care and opening up about myself has always been very hard for me. Being a doctor and caring for other people is not easy, but it's what I am used to. Allowing others to see me, to *really* see me, and learn who I am . . . that's very difficult.

'Since moving to the United States, I have worked very hard. I studied until all hours of the night to get good grades, in order to get into a good university, in order to then get into a good medical school, then to get a good residency, and get a good job. It seems like there was always another reason to put my own needs aside and focus on the goals ahead. But the truth is that I don't even know how to slow down now. And a part of me is scared to.

'Being the "strong one" – the one that gets up early in the morning, gets my kids ready, helps my patients, covers for all my colleagues, helps my parents and my neighbours – that's all I know. Being vulnerable . . . I see how important it can be, but I am also scared that it would slow me down; that it might not let me do everything I do.'

In essence, vulnerability is an open doorway into our very heart. It is the permission to look inside our soul, inviting another to learn the genuine truth about who we are. It makes sense that we might feel vulnerable *about* being vulnerable. And sometimes, slowing down in order to feel and assess our vulnerability feels both foreign and terrifying. Many people share the notion that exploring their vulnerability and emotions in general might slow them down or 'break them'. However, people who do not ever slow down might sometimes crash from burnout. This does not necessarily apply to every single person. However, like the engine light in our vehicles coming on to alert us to the engine needing checking, painful emotions (such as depression, anxiety, irritability and frustration) are usually an indicator that it might be time to check in with ourselves.

According to Brené Brown, the following categories are just some of the examples of situations in which we might feel vulnerable:

- Asking for help
- Noticing our emotions
- Expressing our feelings to others
- Asking someone out
- Sharing a secret
- Initiating sex
- Rejecting sexual advances
- Talking about our weight with others, including medical professionals
- Thinking about our appearance
- Being seen
- Talking about how much money we make
- Talking about our physical illness or food allergies
- Struggling with a mental health disorder

- Having children
- Choosing not to have a child
- Going through trauma, grief or heartbreak
- Feeling disconnected
- Initiating connection
- Feeling unprotected/defenceless and misunderstood

In other words, at all the times that we are in the biggest need for love, support and compassion, we might find ourselves instead feeling ashamed and disconnected, often choosing to hide from the world. There is a common assumption that people have about themselves that if things aren't going well for us, it is our own fault and that we need to 'fix it' in order to be acceptable and lovable again. And yet, if it were a friend going through the same situation, most of us would rush to their side, supporting and reassuring our loved one that they deserve love, support and happiness.

And so, what if this story that we have been telling ourselves about being 'defective' when we are going through a hard time is not the truth? What if the very thing that you try to hide from the world, the very thing you tend to be most ashamed of and feel most vulnerable about, is actually the most lovable thing about you? And what if, when people learned this thing about you, they would not reject you, but rather love you even more? What if they were to thank you for sharing your heart, your truth, your deepest story with them because perhaps they feel the same way?

We tend to tell ourselves the same stories with similar 'I'm not good enough' and 'I don't deserve to be loved' and 'If anyone found this out about me, they would reject me' plot lines. We also live with the 'No, really, you don't understand; in my case, it is absolutely true. I am that one person that would be rejected if people got to know the real me' plot lines. And if you chuckled at this last line, it is probably because this sentence is relatable to you, as it is to me. Because the truth is that we have more commonalities with other people than we have differences and when we are able to be vulnerable with others, we are, in essence, shedding all the layers of our ego and being fully open with another person, allowing us to be fully seen and allowing us to fully see another person too. And that kind of connection is truly magical.

A few years ago, I attended a training seminar, learning the skills of Acceptance and Commitment Therapy (ACT), the principles of which underlie this book. One of the ACT trainers, Dr Steve Hayes, the co-creator of Acceptance and Commitment Therapy, instructed all attendees to put on our name tags. Only instead of our actual names, Dr Hayes requested that we write out our most vulnerable thought, such as 'I am not good enough'.

I remember my hands trembling when I wrote out mine: 'I am an amateur'. I still remember the day I first acquired this label. I was six years old and I had just finished writing my first ever short story. It was a whole five pages! Surely, I thought, it would become a bestseller.

I showed the story to my older brother, who was nearly sixteen at the time and was everyone's definition of 'cool'. He was someone that everyone liked, and everyone wanted to be friends with, and so, his opinion really mattered.

I stood next to him patiently, biting my nails in anticipation, waiting for my big brother to finish reading my story. 'Well, what do you think?' I finally asked him when he was finished.

My brother waved his palm up and down, 'Eh . . . It's kind of amateur.'

My brother was right, of course. I was six. It was my short story. It was the first draft, written in pencil. It was an amateur work of fiction. And yet, that word *amateur* became the fabric behind which I hid my true self for years to come. I wrapped myself in it, as if it defined me. And that day, at that conference, I was able not only to write it out and wear it, I was able to break down the wall behind which I had been hiding for all those years.

The first few hours of wearing the name tag were brutal. Most people at the conference had their hands over their name tags, hiding them, covering them up. I was one of them. However, by lunchtime, something changed. People were mingling and walking up to one another to share their conference experiences, and then inevitably asking to see each other's name tags.

And then something magical happened.

People started finding groups of others who shared a similar name tag, asking about the origin of their story. I remember finding a group of people in which all of us had a version of the 'I'm not good enough' theme, although our exact wording varied, including 'I'm not smart enough', 'I'm not knowledgeable enough', 'I'm not a good enough therapist' and, in my case, 'I am an amateur'. After a while, we all started approaching one another, greeting each other by our name tags, pointing to our own name tag while greeting others, laughing at how similar they all were. 'Hey, Not Good Enough! Me too!'

This experience allowed me to realise the universality of our vulnerability. At its core, it means we build walls to keep people out when we ought to be building bridges to let people in. Because when we accept ourselves, we learn not only to accept but also to love our imperfections. And when that happens, we can finally have the breathing room we need to be who we truly are.

As a process of building our armour of vulnerability, we can practise the Name Tag exercise. For this exercise, you will be asked to write out what your personal name tag would be if you were to put down your most vulnerable thought, one you might typically hide from others. And then, if possible, see if you can recall the story behind the origin of this belief, or perhaps ways in which it has impacted you over the years.

The Name Tag Exercise

I am (insert your name tag)

_____

_____

_____

Story behind this thought or examples of how this belief has impacted my life:

_____

_____

_____

_____

_____

_____

_____

_____

Notice the similarities between these name tags. Clearly, these name tags point not to your true reality but to the reality of your greatest vulnerability. You might fear not being enough and not doing enough, and these thoughts function as a reminder of what you stand for. Remember that you are not your name tag. You are not your trauma. You are not your depression. You are not your thoughts. You are your actions. You are what you stand for. And each and every one of you stands on the side of heroism.

I bring this matter up because when we practise vulnerability and accepting challenging emotions, we also need to practise experiencing joy. The emotion of joy can be a difficult one for many people to experience. For some people, this

Fig. 6

emotion can also activate the feeling of guilt about feeling joyful when others might be suffering. There is an assumption that it is wrong for us to feel happy when other people are going through a hard time, as if our suffering will bring joy to others. The truth is that we have the capacity to experience the entire rainbow of emotions at the same time. This means that we can feel empathy for the suffering of another, the pain of our own traumatic experience or loss, and also joy about a meaningful moment or memory.

Some people might feel afraid of feeling joyful because they might anticipate that if they 'let their guard down' something bad will happen. Brené Brown calls this phenomenon *foreboding joy*.[18] Foreboding joy means that when we experience joy and begin to enjoy this emotion, our anxiety might make us think that this experience is too good to be true and if we are not careful, something bad will happen. Many people, in a superstitious kind of way, believe that the experience of joy might be bad luck and might inadvertently lead to misfortune. In fact, all emotions are fleeting, meaning that all emotions, including happiness, joy and anxiety, are temporary, although we might experience some emotions more frequently than others. However, if after experiencing joy, we later experience sadness, we might sometimes attribute this event to being evidence to support our earlier prediction of misfortune.

Giving yourself the permission to feel joy is one of the most vulnerable experiences you can have. Like floating on water, it

18 Brown, 2015.

requires that at least for a moment, we let go of control and trust the experience. Another way of thinking about emotions is like cookies on a tray. We can have the chocolate chip cookies of joy and connection, and the [insert the name of cookies you don't particularly care for] cookies of sadness and anxiety, and dozens of other types of cookies. You might not like all the cookies on the tray, but you can hold all of them at the same time nonetheless.

Fig. 7

The experience of savouring joy is like taking a bite of one of the cookies. It is true that once you are finished eating the cookie, you might not have another chocolate chip cookie on that tray, but it does not mean that you will never have another cookie of that flavour again. Of course you will. And even though in that moment you might only have one cookie of that kind, you might as well fully enjoy it while you are eating it. In a similar sense, you can give yourself permission to savour joy when it comes. Savour every breath and every bite.

One of my favourite memories of this type occurred a few years ago. I often joke that I am a recovering perfectionist and that I like to plan everything from start to finish. Nothing gives me as much anxiety as being unprepared or running late. That particular trip, I got to experience both.

I was invited to give an eight-hour seminar in Hamburg, Germany. My partner and I flew out from the States. As we landed in Frankfurt, getting ready for our connecting flight to Hamburg, I had my schedule planned out by the minute. We would arrive at Hamburg at 17:00. I would spend two hours preparing and finalising my presentation. Then we would have an early dinner and go to bed by 21:00 in order to get up by 6:00 a.m., have breakfast and get to the seminar room by 7:30 to begin my seminar at 8:00.

When we landed in Frankfurt, however, I discovered (to my horror) that our flight to Hamburg was cancelled due to bad weather. As I was starting to panic, my partner found an attendant at the airport who kindly booked us on to the following flight, which would leave two hours later.

In my mind, I was doing a kind of Tetris-like mathematics – we would arrive at Hamburg at 19:00. I would spend two hours preparing and finalising my presentation. Then we would have a late dinner and go to bed by 23:00 in order to get up by

6:00 a.m., have breakfast and get to the seminar by 7:30 to begin my seminar at 8:00. I spent the next two hours breathing and meditating, my partner assuring me that everything would be OK.

As we went to board the plane to Hamburg for the second time, there was an announcement that all the flights in and out of Frankfurt were now cancelled for the remainder of the day due to bad weather.

Now, I was starting to have a tiny breakdown.

OK, it was an enormous panic attack.

I was in tears.

I was imagining how embarrassing it would be to miss the very talk I had been flown out to do. I was mortified.

The queues to speak to someone were nearly two hours long but my partner found someone who didn't have a queue. Although there were no flights we could get on that day, the kind airport assistant booked us on a train to Hamburg, which would get us there by midnight. The only issue was that the train would be leaving in fifteen minutes from the other end of the airport.

As we ran across the airport, our baggage in our hands, both laughing and crying, we barely made it and were able to board the train.

In my mind, I was again rearranging my schedule – I would prepare my presentation on the train. We would arrive in Hamburg at midnight. We would go to bed by 00:30 and get up by 6:00 a.m., have breakfast and get to the seminar by 7:30 to begin my seminar at 8:00.

I took a little bit of time to prepare and also took a moment to enjoy the gorgeous German countryside with its castles and old churches. I felt like I was on board the *Hogwarts Express*. It was absolutely lovely.

Then two hours into our journey, the train stopped.

There was an announcement in German, and everyone started yelling. When my partner and I found someone who could explain what was going on – a bartender – she explained that there was a fire on the train tracks, and we had to wait until the fire was cleared before the train could move any further.

A fire!

Two and a half hours later, the train started moving backwards. The kind bartender explained that the train was going back to go around the fire but that we were still headed to Hamburg.

At 3:30 a.m., we finally arrived at our station in Hamburg and by 4:00, we finally checked into our hotel and went to sleep, exhausted, jetlagged, only to get up again two hours later.

The following day, as I was teaching my seminar, I was energised and exhausted at the same time. By lunchtime, I had no energy and was running out of steam. My partner brought me a cappuccino. And then there was this moment. This very special moment that I will never forget.

I looked at my partner and really saw him in that moment. Here he was, the love of my life, someone who had been with me the entire time throughout this wild adventure. In my hands was a warm cup of delicious cappuccino. The breeze from the summer air was just lovely. Then my partner looked at me and smiled. And the quiet moment that the two of us shared, just sitting there, smiling at one another, still brings tears to my eyes. It was the purest form of joy and gratitude I had felt in a long time because, in that moment, my mask of perfectionism, overachievement and over-scheduling had fallen off. I was just there. With the love of my life. Sharing a cappuccino and a smile.

I think of this moment often as a reflection of what is truly important in my life. And I think that happiness is not about everlasting moments of joy and glory. I think that happiness is about those little moments of joy, that any bystander might not even fully realise is happening. I think it's watching your kids laugh. I think it's playing with your dog. I think it's about noticing the smile on your loved one's face, the pure smile, the kind that can melt a heart and light the room. To me, these are the pieces that make our vulnerability armour truly magical.

'I guess I have a moment like that,' Shawn says. 'A few years back, there was a fire. We put it out, but this family, they lost everything. I overheard the landlord telling them that it could take months before they could move back in. I looked over and saw this single mom with three kids. She just kept shaking her head, saying, "What are we going to do?"

'My heart broke. I didn't know what to do. I just ran around the corner. My guys shouted at me to see where I was going. I asked them to just give me a minute. I ran around the block to where this pizza joint I used to go to was. I walked in and asked the guy there for a pizza pie to go.

'When I went back, the family was still there. The kids were crying, and the mom looked stunned. I just came by and said, "Here you go, ma'am. It's not a lot but I hope this helps." She looked at me, not understanding. Her kids looked so excited. I wished them well and walked away. When I turned around, as we were all leaving, I saw that she and the kids were eating. It was a moment. The kind that reminded me of why I became a firefighter. I always wish that there is more I could do for people, but that day, I felt like I could offer something.'

Fig. 8: Shawn the Firefighter.

'This is so beautiful,' Hazeem says. 'You have a beautiful soul. For me, before the pandemic, I had a friend, Amir. Amir is retired and is deaf. He could not afford groceries sometimes, so

I asked him to teach me sign language in exchange for free groceries. I have also been studying at home on my own in order to be able to communicate with him. He has not been coming to the store since the pandemic started. I hope he is all right. I will never forget how he smiled when I signed "Hello, my friend, how are you?" to him in Sign Language. When I remember it, my heart feels full. He had tears in his eyes, and he shook my hand, and then he hugged me.'

Chapter 5
The Self-Compassion Potion

As we go through some kind of trauma, tragedy or disaster, as we are trying to glue back the pieces of our own life, inevitably we might be bombarded with additional bad news. We might learn about other tragedies or other people's suffering, or might learn that a valuable system of support that we thought we could count on is suddenly not available. Furthermore, as we are attempting to heal, other people might be needing urgent assistance as well and we might not always have the luxury to put our life or trauma on hold when putting out figurative or literal fires.

Sometimes, as we are dealing with trauma after trauma, not just our own, but seeing the suffering of multiple people around us, such as what happens during the global pandemic or other disasters, we might become completely overwhelmed. After a while, we might feel numb, we might shut down, we might become more irritable and impatient, and sometimes take things out on the people we love the most.

'Yes! That seems exactly how I've been feeling,' Erika says. 'I have been so overwhelmed that I feel like I am just going through the motions during the day. I feel both numb and extremely anxious at the same time. I didn't even know that was possible. I'm also irritable, frustrated and exhausted, with no relief in sight.'

'I definitely noticed that too,' Liz says. 'The other day, I snapped at my mama over the phone, but in reality, I just wished I could hug her through the screen. Seeing my patients and my co-workers suffering is extremely hard but seeing how overwhelmed my mama was feeling this past week hurt my soul. I snapped at her but in reality, I think I was just really sad that I couldn't be with her to support her.'

It makes sense that when we are feeling emotional pain and distress, we might become more irritable and less patient. Behind the shield of anger and frustration, there is usually a gentler, softer emotion of sadness, longing, and a natural human desire to be loved, supported and understood. At the time of a global or national disaster, our own needs might be pushed aside in order to care for the needs of others. And although, at times, this approach might be helpful and even necessary, neglecting our needs for too long can lead to emotional burnout.[1] Burnout is a condition of an extreme feeling of exhaustion, which can also include depression, irritability, numbness, anxiety, sleeplessness or sleeping too much, clumsiness or making mistakes, feelings of anger, conflicts with others, job and relationship dissatisfaction, panic attacks, body tension, headaches, feelings of worthlessness and, in some cases, thoughts of suicide.[2] If not addressed, burnout can lead to worsening mental health symptoms, an overall increased risk of illness due to a compromised

1 Ringenbach, 2009.
2 Dyrbye, et al., 2008; Ringenbach, 2009.

immune system, as well as a heightened risk of diabetes, heart attacks and premature death.[3]

'Oh, I can definitely relate to feeling burned out and struggling with sleeplessness and anxiety. I could work sixteen hours in a row and still have a hard time falling asleep, even though my body was exhausted,' Liz says.

'It makes sense that healthcare professionals and other first responders might feel burned out,' Celeste says. 'I get that, but I don't understand why I am feeling the way that I am. I work a normal forty hours per week. I didn't lose anyone during the pandemic. And yet, I also feel numb and burned out, and now I cry all the time. I just don't understand.'

Just as someone can be physically burned out from working too much, they can also be emotionally burned out from being exposed to a lot of trauma. Even if you do not know anyone who was directly affected by the tragedy, even if you did not lose anyone you knew, the mere impact of the horror of the present situation can have a tremendous impact on how you feel. The reason for that is that most humans are very empathic and seeing other people suffering or learning about the suffering of others (e.g., on the news) can create *empathic distress*. Empathic distress refers to the overwhelming feeling of suffering that we feel when we cannot bear witnessing the suffering of others any longer. As a result, we might experience grief-like or trauma-like symptoms and may wish to withdraw from experiencing any more of such devastating feelings.[4]

3 Ahola, et al., 2010.
4 Dowling, 2018; Klimecki & Singer, 2012.

'I guess this makes sense,' Celeste says. 'I can relate to that, but why does this occur?'

That is a wonderful question. We know that when we see someone else suffering, we are likely to feel empathy towards them. In fact, if you have ever witnessed anyone in front of you, or perhaps on a television screen, eating a lemon, you might have experienced salivation in your mouth and perhaps even a shadow of a slightly sour taste in your mouth.[5] Sometimes, even reading about lemons is enough to cause this reaction.

Our ability for empathy allows us to understand what the other person might be tasting when they are eating a lemon. Furthermore, our memories of our own past experiences of eating lemons might also affect how we experience watching others eat a lemon. For example, if you hate lemons, you might also experience disgust when seeing other people eat lemons, but if you love lemons, you might feel a pleasant taste in your mouth, even though you are not actually eating a lemon yourself. What this means is that if you have already experienced a lot of grief, loss and trauma in the past, you are more likely to be impacted by seeing other people suffering because you might remember what it felt like for you to suffer in the past. This is why even seeing fictional characters going through abuse, loss and trauma can be triggering and painful if we have been through similar experiences ourselves.

Our brains are prewired for empathy in order to help us to maintain connections with other people and maximise our

5 Hagenmuller, et al., 2014.

chances of survival. Not too long ago, scientists discovered *mirror neurons*, a kind of nerve cell in the brain that becomes active both when we engage in a particular task ourselves, such as dancing, and when we watch other people perform the same task.[6] The same applies when we experience a particular emotion (such as grief or anger) or see someone else experience the same emotion. However, the process of empathy is not merely 'emotion contagion'. It is not a mere imitation of what another person does or feels, but instead, it is our own interpretation of what the other individual might be feeling or doing based on our own past experiences. So, when we see or read about another person grieving over the death of a loved one, we might remember how awful it was when we went through a similar loss. And just like the stranger whom we are reading about, we too are likely to grieve at that moment.

Our devastating and traumatic experiences can stay in our body. As trauma expert, Bessel van der Kolk says in his ground-breaking book *The Body Keeps the Score*, our past unprocessed traumas stay locked in our body until one day we might find the key to safely open up the door and experience the painful emotions stored in there in a safe and supportive way.[7] So, it is possible that for many of us, seeing and reading about the devastation that other people are going through is bringing up our own pain, and, as a result, causing us to experience empathic distress. Until we are able to process the pain that shows up in

6 Berrol, 2006.
7 van der Kolk, 2014.

the moments of empathic distress and at the times that we feel triggered, we might not be able to move past it.

'But how do you open this door without breaking?' Hazeem asks. 'I feel as if there is a dam of grief inside of me. And if I open that door, I fear that I will not be able to face it. When my father died . . . I still cannot talk about it . . . I . . . do not know if I can do this.'

Of course, it makes sense that facing our past grief and trauma will seem daunting and terrifying. The truth is that the pain we are afraid to face is there whether or not we agree to face it. However, there is a way that we can face it gradually, over time. In order for us to truly be able to face these experiences, we would need to learn how to create a sense of emotional safety for ourselves. This means that we don't have to dive fully into our deepest darkest traumatic experiences on the first try. Trauma processing is not the Olympics, which means that we do not need to compete with anyone else, not even with ourselves. Trauma processing is a practice, which means that you cannot get it wrong and it is perfectly OK to go at your own pace. Self-compassion researchers Kristin Neff and Chris Germer discuss the concept of 'Opening and Closing' in their powerful workbook *The Mindful Self-Compassion Workbook*, which I highly recommend.[8] The concept of 'Opening and Closing' refers to allowing our hearts and our emotions to be as open as we feel safe for them to be. This means allowing ourselves to be very gradual with this process and allowing ourselves to

8 Neff & Germer, 2018.

close and take 'time off' from trauma processing in order to rest and recover. This kind of emotional safety building is vital for trauma processing in order to allow us to learn to associate the process of trauma processing with safety.

One way to do that is through observing what you are feeling, normalising it, and then offering physical and emotional soothing for yourself. These steps are similar to Kristin Neff's three components of self-compassion.[9] Let's review and practise these steps now.

Step 1: Name and observe it. This means observing and naming your experience. For example, if you are watching a movie in which a character is going through a similar traumatic experience to yours, you might in some cases notice yourself feeling overwhelmed and tense. You might feel triggered and you might experience an emotional flashback. Recall that an emotional flashback is a feeling of trauma related to emotions in your body even if you are not cognitively thinking of your traumatic experience at that time (see Chapter 3).[10]

In order to practise the first step, you can name this experience. For example, 'I am feeling triggered. I am experiencing an emotional flashback. I feel tense. I am noticing that I am holding my breath. My heart is beating fast. I feel dizzy and unsafe.'

Step 2: Normalise it. Acknowledge that it makes sense that you are feeling this way. Whether you are feeling sad, angry,

9 Neff, 2011.
10 Walker, 2013.

devastated or unsafe, your emotions make sense and all your emotions are allowed and valid.

Remind yourself that people all over the world are experiencing the same symptoms in similar situations. Your reaction is completely normal and makes perfect sense given your history and your experiences.

'Hmm, I was always taught that we shouldn't get angry,' Liz says. 'I know you mentioned before that all emotions, including anger, can be informative. But anger specifically is hard for me because I was taught that that emotion is a bad thing to feel and that we shouldn't allow ourselves to get angry.'

This point comes up a lot when we are talking about feeling our emotions, especially anger. The truth is that there are no 'bad emotions'. You are allowed to feel any and all of them. Emotions are not the same thing as actions. The emotion of anger is not the same as an action of violence, although the two often get confused. You are also allowed to feel sad, jealous, insecure, frustrated, scared, happy, exhilarated, and any emotion in the world at any time.

Step 3: Soothe yourself. Just as you would soothe and support a dear friend or a small child, see how you can support yourself in that moment, both physically and emotionally. Soothing yourself with kindness in a moment of grief is like hugging someone at a funeral – it will not bring back the deceased, but it can offer support to the survivor of this loss. In a similar manner, you can offer yourself emotional comfort too. You can do this by hugging yourself, placing your hands on your heart centre, holding a hot beverage in your hands or against your heart centre (over your clothes), cuddling your pet or a stuffed animal, wrapping a blanket around yourself, or hugging a pillow against your chest and stomach. The idea behind these practices is to help your body to soothe and stimulate the production of oxytocin: the soothing chemical.

In addition to supporting yourself physically, you can also practise soothing yourself emotionally. This means that after naming and observing (Step 1) and normalising (Step 2) your experiences, you can also offer some compassionate reassurance and support for yourself. For example, you can say to yourself, 'I know this is very hard right now. I've been through this before. I can get through this again. I might not *feel* safe right now, but right now, in this moment, I am physically safe.'[11] In addition, you can try using different pronouns, such as 'we' or 'you'. For example, 'I've got you. You are safe.' Or, 'We are going to get through this. We are OK.' Everyone has a different preference, whatever phrases and pronouns you prefer; they are all OK to use.

You are allowed to feel safe and supported in your own way. For some people, this practice entails curling up in the blanket for a few hours or taking a nap. For others, self-soothing means going for a walk or a run. For other people, this practice means cuddling up with a loved one, whereas for others, it means allowing some time to themselves for a while. Whatever

---

11 If you are not physically safe, get to safety as soon as possible before continuing these exercises.

your method of self-soothing is, it is perfectly OK if it can help you to better cope with what you are going through.

'This sounds so nice,' Erika says. 'But this is also very hard for me. I'm good at being there for others, but not for myself. I don't usually find the time to do something nice for myself. It feels selfish somehow and, in any case, I have no time for it.'

'I agree that it feels selfish,' Shawn says. 'It seems strange to be taking care of myself when so many others are suffering out there.'

Self-compassion appears to be very challenging for a lot of people and this is at least in part due to the many misconceptions about it. Most people believe that self-compassion equates to selfishness, laziness, self-pitying or overindulgence. However, research studies are finding the complete opposite effects.[12] When we are able to practise self-compassion, we are likely to be less selfish and more productive than if we keep pushing ourselves beyond our limits. Just think of how you treat others when you are sleep-deprived, exhausted and hungry, as compared to when you are well rested and well fed. Self-compassion is essentially an investment in your health, in your energy, in activating your inner superpowers, and in you being more effective at what you do. If you have ever flown on an aeroplane, you might remember the flight attendants' instructions to 'put on your own mask' before you assist others around you. Well, never has the idea of putting on your own mask before

12 Neff, 2004; Neff & Dahm, 2015.

helping others been more true than it is today. Only in addition to the literal sense of wearing a mask, it also means taking a moment to recharge, even if it is just taking three slow mindful breaths every hour as your very own self-compassion 'on the go' practice.

Another misconception about self-compassion is that it equates to feeling sorry for yourself (self-pity) or allowing others to feel sorry for you. However, self-compassion and self-pity are actually very different from one another. Whereas the concept of self-pity implies that we are alone in feeling the way that we are feeling, the concept of self-compassion normalises our experiences in reminding us that our feelings are universal and that most people would be feeling the way that we are feeling if they were to be in the same situation.[13]

'I don't necessarily feel self-pity,' Celeste says, 'but I often think that I am lazy and that I am over-indulging when I'm staying in and not going outside. I find that I often shame myself for not going outside. I keep thinking that I'm not doing enough and that I'm just being lazy.'

This is a great point. Self-compassion is often confused with overindulgence; however, the two are actually different from one another. Whereas indulgence is avoidance-based, self-compassion is a needed break in order to allow you to *return* to face your responsibilities. Hence, self-compassion is meant to support you while you're experiencing your emotions, rather than to allow you to avoid processing them altogether. For

13 Neff, 2004; Neff & Dahm, 2015.

example, taking a nap for a little while in order to rest and be able to do your work is perfectly OK, whereas sleeping for several days so that you don't feel the pain of your loss will likely not be helpful towards your healing in the long term.

Celeste thinks about it. 'Hmm, I guess my behaviours started out as self-compassion and then turned into avoidance over time. I want to overcome this but I'm really having a hard time. I keep telling myself that tomorrow I'm going to go to the store, that tomorrow I won't engage in any compulsions, I really try. And then when "tomorrow" comes, I just can't seem to do it. I feel terrible. I feel like I've become lazy. I shame myself all the time.'

'Me too,' Erika says. 'I shame myself too for everything, but it seems like no matter what I do, it's never enough. I think I'm not doing enough either for my patients or for my family; it's never enough. And so, I'm always working, and I never allow myself to rest.'

Many of us use harsh, critical and shaming voices to motivate ourselves. We might call ourselves 'lazy' or other hurtful names. We might criticise our work, our appearance, our abilities, our illness, our trauma, as well as our need to rest and our very human need to be treated with love and compassion. Many people mistakenly believe that if they are hard on themselves, they will work harder to reach their goals, and that if they treat themselves with compassion, they will stop trying to succeed and become lazy. It is true that harsh criticism can motivate us to work hard . . . at least initially. However, when we (inevitably) have a setback, as everyone else in the world has setbacks, we are more likely to be discouraged and want to give up. But what if our setbacks were to be met with self-compassion and understanding, not in the way of being 'let off the hook' but in a way of understanding that doing well is important to you and you might like to try again.

Think of it like a video game. Whenever we complete a level, we might feel pretty good about ourselves. But when we level up, we are likely to run into new challenges and possibly lose several times before we learn how to defeat the current game level and level up once more. Everyone makes mistakes. They are how we learn and how we get better.

'I hear what you are saying,' Erika says, 'but I am a doctor, I can't make mistakes.'

'I was thinking the same thing,' Liz says. 'I make a mistake, people die.'

Of course, it makes sense that mistakes, especially in any medical or first-responder work, are to be avoided at all costs. Practising complacency would not be helpful and could even be harmful. This is exactly why we are talking about self-compassion. Research studies have actually found that heightened burnout rates are associated with a significantly heightened risk of medical errors.[14] This means that if you are working in any kind of life-saving profession, self-compassion is even more important because it can help to reduce your burnout, allowing you to remain the superhero that you are. It also means that although we all understandably want to avoid

14 Shanafelt, et al., 2010; Tawfik, et al., 2018.

making mistakes, the way that we treat ourselves when any kind of mistakes arise makes a difference.

'If I ever make a mistake,' Liz says, 'even if it's not about work, I lay into myself. I really shame myself, sometimes for days.'

'Me too,' Erika says.

Let's do a practice exercise. I would like to invite you to think about a recent mistake you have made. Please don't choose the worst mistake you believe you have ever made, but perhaps a moderate-level one. So, if we were to rate the severity of our perceived mistakes from 1 to 10, 10 being the worst mistake we have ever made, see if you can think of a 3–4 level mistake. Once you think about it, please write down not the details of the mistake but the self-critical judgements you have/had towards yourself about making this mistake. In other words, please write down whatever your self-critic was telling you about yourself. If at all possible, see if you would be willing to write out what you said to yourself in as much detail as possible. You can write it below or on a separate piece of paper, if you wish, or on your electronic device.

_____

_____

_____

_____

_____

_____

_____

_____

_____

'It was a little rough, but I was able to finish it,' Erika says.

Great! Now I am going to invite you to read the letter out loud, only I am going to ask you to imagine that you are actually addressing your child, your spouse, your best friend, or someone from this group instead.

Erika looks stunned. 'Wait, are you serious? I . . . I don't think I can.' She breathes for a few minutes and then tears begin running down her face. 'This is horrible. I just imagined reading it to my oldest daughter . . . and I just couldn't imagine talking to her this way. I imagined the look of pain on her precious face . . . I . . . can't . . . I can't even read it.'

This is sadly true for so many of us. The harsh tone with which we might address ourselves would be likely considered abusive if we were to apply it to someone else. And so, if speaking this way to another would be considered abusive or an act of bullying, then it makes sense that bullying ourselves might be too extreme a form of punishment for most mistakes a human might make.

'So, how do I get rid of these critical thoughts?' Erika asks.

So often, we might judge and criticise ourselves for struggling, for being scared, for feeling overwhelmed, for not knowing how to handle a certain situation, including a global pandemic or a terrorist attack, something we were not trained or prepared to handle. And so, at the times that we are judging ourselves with severity and harshness, we can imagine ourselves as a small child. Perhaps remembering the innocent, lovable little child you once were, and seeing if one day, you might be able to see the innocent, lovable adult that you are now. However, if practising self-compassion towards yourself even in a child form is too painful or challenging, see if you can see yourself as a separate person, as another individual who is struggling in this way. Or perhaps imagine that it is your loved one who is going through this challenge.

Although we know that trying to 'get rid of' our thoughts or feelings is a losing battle, we can over time learn to face and even befriend our thoughts and feelings. In order to do that, we need to get to know our monsters. Typically, we do all that we can to run away from them, but what if we assume that the monsters only appear threatening because they are themselves threatened, that perhaps they are frightening because *they* are frightened?

I have two cats, and one of them, Vader, likes to play a game of tag with me. When we are playing this game, I chase Vader around the house until he runs into a corner and can't run any further. Just then, he turns around and faces me and I run away. Then Vader chases me around the house until I run into a corner, only to turn around and chase him again.

When we keep running away from our feelings, we don't get a chance to get to know them. But what if instead of running away, we stop running, turn around, and face them?

Let's try it out. See if you can answer the questions below in order to get to know, and possibly befriend, your monsters:

1) Who are your monsters? Anxiety? Shame? Insecurity? Depression?

_____

_____

_____

2) Pick one of these monsters for the purpose of this exercise. What is the monster telling you? What are some of its messages?

_____

_____

_____

3) If we assume, for a moment, that the monster is not malevolent, but instead is actually just misguided and misunderstood; if we assume that the monster is acting out because of its own unmet need, then what might the monster need? Attention/love/support?

_____

_____

_____

4) If we also assume that the monster's criticism is actually a misguided attempt to protect you, what might the monster be trying to protect you from? Criticism from others? Rejection? Failure?

_____

_____

_____

5) If you can take a few moments to reassure and support your monster, see if you can thank it for looking out for you and see if you can give your monster some reassurance. For example, 'Thanks, anxiety, but I've got this.'

_____

_____

_____

'This was definitely a different way of looking at it,' Liz says. 'I was not surprised to see that my inner critic was trying to protect me from failure and rejection, but I was surprised about how much gentler it felt to see it as a well-intentioned monster rather than a malevolent one.'

'I saw that my monster was trying to protect me from being complacent,' Shawn says, 'but even with that, I find that self-compassion overall is very hard for me. I just don't feel like I deserve it.'

For most people, it is easier to feel and demonstrate compassion towards others than it is to be compassionate towards themselves.[15] In fact, one way we can include ourselves in a self-compassionate practice could be by initially cultivating compassion towards others. We can practise compassion towards our loved ones, strangers or even fictional characters. Let's try an example of this practice now:

15 Neff, 2011.

Compassion Towards Another Superhero

Everyone goes through a hard time sometimes. Batman, Superman and Wonder Woman have all lost people they loved and cared about. Every person, real and fictional, feels sad, scared or overwhelmed sometimes.

I'd like you to think of a real-life hero, or perhaps a super-hero or another fictional character, who has ever felt sad or scared. What was going on in that situation? Write about it or draw it in the space below.

Can you name the emotions that character might have been going through?

_____

_____

_____

What would you say to this character if you could actually talk to them in that situation? Write about it or draw your response in the space below.

Have you ever known anyone else who felt emotions similar to those this character has felt? If yes, imagine that you could say something to support that person; what would you say?

_____

_____

_____

Have you ever felt that way too? Do you ever experience similar emotions – feeling sad, scared or overwhelmed? If so, what do you think you could say to yourself in the same caring way that you treated the hero you wrote about? Write about it or draw your response in the space below.

'This was interesting,' Liz says. 'I wrote about Rosa Parks. She's one of my biggest heroes. My nana actually met her a few times. I always knew that Rosa Parks was incredibly courageous for what she did, for her role in the Civil Rights Movement. But I have never thought about how hard it must have been for her. I mean, logically I realised that it wasn't easy, but I never previously considered that she might have felt scared or anxious. I don't actually know how she felt but I imagined how I would have felt in that situation. Feeling that anxiety and still going through with it, standing up to every single person on that bus, that's . . . that's courageous. That is what I aspire to be.'

'You might not see it yet,' Shawn says, 'but you already are. Courageous, I mean. Everything that you have been through, everything that you have chosen to do, everything that you do on a daily basis – that's courage. I imagine that your nana would have been proud. I imagine that Rosa Parks would have been, too.'

Liz smiles. 'Thanks, Shawn. That's very kind of you.'

'For me,' Shawn says, 'I thought of Batman in this exercise. Batman's always been my favourite. It was powerful to think of him in this way. It made me want to be there for him, to support him.'

And in a similar way as you would support your favourite hero, your hero can also support you, even if through an exercise. So, if you are willing, take a few moments to think of a personal hero. A personal hero is someone you see as a figure of ultimate wisdom and compassion. This could be a real person, such as a grandparent, a teacher, a mentor, a star athlete you admire, a creator or a historical figure you look up to. This person can be living or deceased. Or, your hero can be a fictional character, such as Spider-Man, Harry Potter, Professor Dumbledore or Wonder Woman.

If you cannot think of a personal hero, that's perfectly OK, see if you can think of a kind of hero you'd like to have or look up to. What kind of qualities would your hero have? You can always think of Batman as a default.

_____
_____
_____

Now, take a few moments to imagine that you have some alone time with your hero. Your hero knows exactly what you have been through, what your origin story is, and how it has shaped you. Your hero is understanding, supportive and encouraging. Your hero knows exactly what to say to you and what you need to hear.

What would your hero say to you?

If it is too difficult to think of what your hero might say, no problem. It happens to a lot of people. Take a breath. You can always try this exercise at another time.

_____

_____

_____

_____

_____

_____

_____

_____

_____

'Aww, this was very sweet,' Erika says. 'It wasn't easy, but it was very sweet, too.'

'I was nearly in tears,' Celeste says. 'I imagined one of my favourite characters from an anime. He is a very caring and compassionate teacher who never gives up on his students, no matter what. In this exercise, the sensei (the teacher) sat down next to me and reminded me of how much I have been through and how hard I have worked my entire life. He said regardless of how my parents treated me, that he was proud of me, and that he believes in me. He was kind and understanding and he said that when I am ready to practise leaving the house on a more regular basis, he would be there by my side ... I know it was just an imaginary exercise, but I didn't realise until now how much I needed to hear those words.'

'Thank you so much for sharing, my friends,' Hazeem says. 'This was a very sweet exercise for me also. I ... I spoke with my father ...' He sniffles and takes a breath. 'He sat down with me. I was a little boy again. He put his arm around me and ... he said he is still with me ... He said that I honour him with my actions, and ...' He dabs his eyes. 'And that he will always guide me, whenever I need. It was ... it was what I really needed to hear right now.' He nods and smiles at the same time.

We have all been through a lot. Our losses, traumas and tragedies do not make us broken. They make us valuable, learned and wise. These experiences may be painful, but they also give us the wisdom of how to support ourselves and others in a similar situation in the future. In Japan, there exists the practice of Kintsugi (金継ぎ, which means 'golden joinery').

In the practice of Kintsugi, when a piece of pottery, such as a bowl, breaks, it is not discarded. Instead, the bowl would be mended, and rather than hiding its cracks, they are accentuated with gold lacquer. Bowls and other articles mended in this way are considered to be very valuable, something to be cherished and treated with respect and care.

Fig. 9: Kintsugi (golden joinery).

Just as we would care for a cherished collectible item in our house, so we can treat ourselves and our bodies with the same level of reverence and care. This means allowing ourselves the ability to rest, eat, slow down and sleep when we need to, as well as the ability to set boundaries with ourselves and others, because being a hero on a daily basis is exhausting. Whether you work in a hospital, care for a family member, support your co-workers or just battle your own dragons on a daily basis, you need to be able to have some time to recharge.

Think about how we treat our mobile devices. When our mobile is running out of battery, we plug it in and let it recharge. Even superheroes deserve a little break in order to supercharge their batteries. For example, Superman goes to the Fortress of Solitude when he needs some time to himself, and Batman has an entire Batcave of his own.

Like Batman and Superman, we all need to visit our own sanctuary sometimes. A sanctuary is a safe space in which we can rest and regain our energy. It can be a corner in your room, or a pillow on the floor, or a tree that you visit outside. Alternatively, your sanctuary can be a fully imagined place, which you can visit in your mind.

Let's try to brainstorm some ideas for a potential sanctuary that you might like. If you could design your own safe space, your own sanctuary, what would it look like? What items would be in that place? Perhaps books, games, pillows or colouring books would be there, or maybe your dog or cat would also accompany you in there?

What are some ways in which you can create such a place for yourself in even the smallest capacity? For example, arranging a few books and pillows on the floor to create a small safe space for yourself.

'Aww, this felt so nice,' Erika says. 'I imagined myself on a beach with my husband and kids. It sounds so tempting right now. I think I really need a vacation. My husband and I both work very hard, often without days off, but once per year we take a vacation to unwind and relax. Over the past year, we did not take a vacation. I think I am overdue.'

'A vacation on the beach sounds very nice,' Celeste says. 'My image was just sitting in a café with my wife and my friends. I just miss that – hanging out and laughing with other people. There is something really lovely about that image.'

As important as it is for us to have a sanctuary, it can be equally important to practise setting boundaries with other people. Setting boundaries with others refers to the practice of saying 'no' to new assignments, responsibilities and requests when you are burning out and not getting enough time to rest or recover. In addition, this practice includes making requests, such as asking for support or additional assistance.

Here are a few examples of boundary setting with others:

- 'Thank you for approaching me about taking on this project. Normally, I would be happy to take it on. However, my plate is unfortunately completely full at the moment. Thank you for understanding.'
- 'Unfortunately, I am unable to help you today, but I can help you tomorrow.'
- 'I am noticing that I am burning out and feeling over-whelmed. It would be very helpful to receive additional assistance or an extension with this project.'

In a similar manner, we can also practise setting boundaries with ourselves. This means not allowing our inner critic and our sense of overachievement to control our behaviour. Here are a few examples of boundary setting with ourselves:

- 'I know that you feel compelled to take on this project but it is best for your mental and physical health to turn it down.'
- 'I know that you feel obligated to help your friend move to his new home but it is OK for you to let him know that you have been in a lot of pain and might not be able to help him.'
- 'I know that you think that you have to clean the entire house every time your friends come to visit but because of your health, it might not be helpful for you to clean so much. It is OK to have your friends over even if you do not vacuum all the carpets and wash all the dishes.'
- 'I realise that I am mad at myself for making this mistake, but I am also a person and I will not allow myself to be shamed in this way.'

'I see how setting boundaries is really important and I certainly also feel guilty whenever I try to set them,' Erika says. 'However, last week, I actually took a half-day with my family and just relaxed for a while. I really enjoyed it and clearly really needed it, but I also felt guilty for experiencing joy while others are struggling in the world.'

It makes sense that it might be very challenging to experience joy while others are suffering. And also, allowing yourself to feel joy does not take away from the situation itself. Your allowing yourself to feel joy (and any other emotions that you might experience) can make you more resilient to support yourself and also to show up for the rest of the world. So, go ahead. Take some time for yourself. Recharge. Power up. You've earned it. And then come back and help save the world.

Chapter 6
Your Heroic Sense of Purpose

My palms still feel clammy every time I think about that day. I was driving home from work after a particularly challenging day. A co-worker had exploded at me for asking her if she was OK. One of my clients failed to show up to our appointment. And, as a clinical trainee, I was sure that I was doing everything wrong. I felt humiliated and defeated. I thought about quitting my job, believing myself to be not good enough at it and day-dreaming about a calmer environment in which I would not have to worry about making mistakes and in which I would not be responsible for other people's lives. It wasn't that I hated my job. I loved it. But the fear of making a mistake and doing something wrong kept me up at night, causing tremendous anxiety.

I would meet with my supervisor more frequently than I was supposed to, double-checking every detail with her. And no matter how many times she reassured me that I was doing a good job, I believed myself to be the worst therapist that ever lived. I read as many treatment manuals as I could get my hands on, attended multiple trainings and conferences, but the Imposter Syndrome was still there. No matter what I did, I could not get rid of it. I tried meditating, I tried resting more, I tried avoiding anything, including things I liked, such as going out to meet a friend, on the off chance that it would worsen my anxiety.

And so, on that particular day, as I was driving home and thinking about how I wanted not to feel this tremendous anxiety any more, I got hit with the worst panic attack I had ever had. My vision started blurring. I felt like I couldn't breathe. I was cold and sweating at the same time. And I couldn't stop hyperventilating and shaking.

It seemed as if the accumulated anxiety of my whole lifetime had decided to explode all at the same time.

I knew that it was a panic attack, but I did not want to experience it. I got off the freeway, imagining that I would just walk home if I had to, even though home was still over 30 miles away. But my anxiety was so severe, there was no way that I could keep driving.

And then my phone rang. It was my friend. Let's call her 'Lisa'. Answering the phone (hands free), I asked her if everything was all right. But it wasn't.

Lisa was about to kill herself.

I asked her to please just wait until I got there and I got back on the freeway. I was still scared, still panicking, but my fear was now irrelevant. I had a mission and my mission had my focus: help my friend.

We stayed on the phone until I got there, and I assisted her with getting psychiatric assistance and contacting her loved ones. She went through several treatments and is doing much better now. What she doesn't know is that she was the one that saved me that day. By reaching out to me and trusting me, she allowed me to focus on something bigger than my anxiety, on something bigger than myself. She helped me to remember that if a client doesn't show up to a session 'it's not about me', and chances are that something might be going on in that person's life. She helped me to reconnect with my sense of purpose of helping people, and she helped me to bring my focus back towards what really mattered to me, what has always mattered to me. Don't get me wrong, I still have the Imposter Syndrome. I have it right now, as I am typing this sentence for this book. But realising what my sense of purpose is has allowed me to take steps towards it even when I am anxious.

'I didn't realise there was a name for it,' Shawn says. 'I have certainly felt my fair share of this and still do.'

'I remember when I graduated nursing school,' Liz says. 'I was sure that I was an imposter and that someone was going to find out. I remember when I had to take care of a patient by myself for the first time. And now, as I work from home and many people's lives are in my hands, I still feel like an imposter. Logically, I know that I'm not, but this feeling is very prevalent.'

'I don't know if this would be called the Imposter Syndrome,' Celeste says, 'but I think it's more like I don't feel like I can contribute in any way to helping people because I'm not a doctor or a nurse.'

'I feel the same way too,' Hazeem says. 'There is always more I would like to be able to do and I still do not feel like I am doing enough to help people.'

Many people think that they have to have a certain job, a certain amount of money or other resources in order to be able to help people. However, we are always capable of doing something, even if that something is different from the way that we initially thought. This is where a little imagination can go a very long way. For example, have you ever wished that you could be part of a fictional universe, like the DC or Marvel universes, the *Supernatural* universe, Harry Potter's Wizarding World or *Star Wars'* galaxy far, far away? Have you ever wondered what you would do if you had certain superpowers or magical abilities? Have you thought what you might do if you could help other people? Well, here is your chance. You do not have to wait to live your life. This is your moment.

YOU ARE THE CHOSEN ONE. This is your journey, your adventure and your call to action. It has to be you. You are the only one who can be the kind of superhero that we need at this time. And every superhero has a sense of purpose.

Your sense of purpose essentially refers to the kind of person that you would like to be. It refers to your core – what matters most to you. Core values stem from acceptance and commitment therapy and essentially refer to the categories of what you care about.[1] For example, you might care about helping people, as well as about being a good friend or a social justice advocate; perhaps you care about creativity, travel, health, learning, being a part of your family (blood, relationship or a chosen one), your fandom, your support group or other association.

Values are different from goals. Whereas goals are finite, meaning that you can cross them off after you have achieved them, core values are infinite.[2] For example, graduating from a university might be a goal, whereas education and learning are

1 Hayes, 2019.
2 Hayes, 2019.

both core values. Similarly, getting groceries for your immuno-compromised neighbour might be a goal, whereas helping people is a core value. Your core values are essentially a map for your sense of purpose, a map for your heroic quest.

There are numerous ways of exploring your sense of purpose. Here we are going to explore seven of them:

1. What do you stand for? Many people believe that in order to live a good life, they must always *feel* happy and joyful. However, both happiness and joy are fleeting emotions, which means that they come and go. Happiness essentially means feeling satisfied, feeling content and feeling pleasure. For example, you might feel happy after being promoted, after receiving an award or when relaxing on the beach. On the other hand, joy refers to a heartfelt moment of connection with a meaningful person, animal or an activity that we genuinely love and care about. For example, watching kids playing and laughing can bring tears to our eyes in the moment of pure joy. Mindfully spending time with people we care about can also make our heart fill with joy.

Perhaps the main difference between happiness and joy is that happiness is said to be a *hedonic* experience, whereas joy is believed to be a *eudaimonic* experience.[3] The hedonic (from the word 'hedonism') experience is one that relies on pleasure, such as gifts, good food, achievements, good music and other pleasurable experiences. On the other hand, the eudaimonic

3 Ryan & Deci, 2001.

experience of joy refers to the connection to our sense of purpose, such as being present with loved ones, helping others, being selfless and focusing on the picture greater than ourselves. And although both emotions tend to be short lasting, and although both can contribute to our 'feeling good', they don't necessarily feel the same. Specifically, the emotions of joy can occur on their own and also in a mixture with other (sometimes painful) emotions, such as grief. For example, spending time with a dying family member can activate both grief and immense joy. Helping a friend through the death of a spouse can bring up a mixture of feelings, such as grief, empathy, love and joy. So, in essence, it means that although both happiness and joy are important, focusing on chasing these emotions might take us away from our meaningful journey. And so, rather than spending our life chasing happiness, we can think about what it is we want to stand for. We might not always feel 'good' in the moment, but perhaps 'feeling good' might not be the goal we need to set in the first place. Perhaps then, living a full life is not about avoiding what we don't want, such as anxiety, grief, etc. But rather about doing what's important *regardless* of the obstacles that might show up.

2. Intense emotions are a source of information. Sometimes, our sense of purpose brings our pain and fear and sometimes it comes from it. Sometimes, doing the right thing means facing our inner dragons and at other times, we might become more driven to show up for a given cause because of the painful experience that we went through.

'This makes sense,' Shawn says. 'In my case, it was because of 9/11 that I decided to become a firefighter.'

'Same,' Liz says. 'It was after 9/11 and after Hurricane Katrina that I decided I wanted to go into healthcare. However, I still never feel like I am doing enough.'

Interestingly, our emotions – especially intense emotions – tend to point to what we care about most. In fact, the inverse of your greatest fears usually points to your greatest sense of purpose. For example, if you fear rejection and criticism, it likely means that you value connection and belonging. If you fear failure or being inadequate, it likely suggests that you care about being good at what you do. Rather than trying to escape from your fear monsters, use them as your own roadmap to your sense of purpose. Take actions to honour this core value regardless of any monsters you might encounter on the way.

Here is an exercise to help you identify your sense of purpose based on your fears and anxieties:

A): Identify some of your biggest fears or frustrations (for example, fears of losing a loved one, being rejected or criticised, making a mistake, getting sick or dying, or frustration over people not being kind to one another, anger over people not following rules or acting in a hateful manner).

_____

_____

_____

_____

_____

B): Turn your emotions around as an indicator of what you care about.

For example, if you fear getting rejected, it might mean that you care about connection, belonging and acceptance.

If you fear losing a loved one, it might mean that this loved one is very important to you and you care about spending time with them.

If you fear getting sick or dying, it might be because there are still many things you wish to do in this life.

If you are angry about injustices in the world, it could mean that you care about equality, compassion and social justice.

_____
_____
_____
_____
_____

C): Identify small steps you can take to participate in activities that you care about.

For example, if you realised that you care about acceptance and connection, it might mean spending some time with people you want to remain connected to.

_____
_____
_____
_____
_____

***

'I really care about helping people,' Shawn says. 'But when it seems as though I am unable to help others, I get really down on myself. My sense of purpose seems to be centred around doing what I can to help others. I have been thinking of ways to support my friends and my guys at the station. There are definitely things I would like to do.'

'I want to help others too,' Liz says. 'I realise that I have been so used to thinking of helping others medically that I hadn't considered that there are other ways that I can help others. I would like to focus on amplifying the voices of Black and Indigenous individuals, and People of Colour, as well as women, gender minorities, LGBTQIA individuals and others whose rights have been frequently violated. I want to advocate for their rights. I want to give them a voice. I want to make sure that what happened to my grandmother doesn't happen to anyone else.'

'Hmm, I have not previously considered that to this extent,' Erika says, 'but I would like to stand up for myself at work. I am definitely burning out and I am tired of being treated differently than my male colleagues.'

And as we saw, we can use our emotions as roadmaps to our sense of purpose. Here are a few examples of how others have been able to do so:

After years of being bullied in her high school, Juanita (not her real name) wanted to do something about it. Feeling powerless and scared was a familiar feeling and Juanita did not think she was able to do much to help herself or others. However, when seeing another student in her school getting bullied, Juanita had an idea. She wrote that student a supportive note on a sticky paper and posted the note on the student's locker. But right as she was posting it, Juanita had a moment of epiphany – if one student could benefit from receiving a supportive note, couldn't all students benefit? She then spent several hours posting supportive sticky notes on every single student's locker. The effect of this heroic gesture was incredible. Students reported feeling supported, loved and seen, and over time, the amount of bullying in her school significantly reduced. Just one action can have a tremendous effect on how others feel and act sometimes, and in Juanita's case, her one act of kindness had an incredible effect on the feelings and behaviours of many.

Similar to Juanita, a little boy named Ewan also set out to make a difference. Ewan realised that there were countless homeless individuals in Detroit, Michigan, many of whom had no food and no warm clothes to support them during the winter. So, at seven years old, little Ewan asked his mother if they could make a few peanut butter and jelly sandwiches for the individuals who needed food. His mom agreed. Soon, Ewan's efforts became publicly known and now there are weekly trucks that help Ewan both collect and distribute food and warm clothes to the homeless individuals in Detroit. Ewan goes by the name Super Ewan now and wears a distinctive superhero cape, for he truly is a real-life superhero.[4]

4 Culp, 2017.

So, what is the cause you care about? Is it justice? Equality? Mental health awareness? Health awareness, including mask safety? Or perhaps you care about the creativity and humour that we all need in order to remember that there is also a light when everything else seems dark? Perhaps you care about education and educating others?

You might not be able to change everything overnight, but you can be the force towards the change in that direction. So whether it is posting a supportive message on social media for others whenever you feel overwhelmed, helpless and depressed, or checking on your friends when you feel lonely, or taking some time to support yourself so that you can show up to support others, taking a step towards your sense of purpose creates ripples that can forever change not only your own life, but perhaps the lives of countless others that you affect for the better.

3) Consider your legacy. How do you want to be remembered after you have died? That's a sobering question, isn't it? What would you want people to say about you in your eulogy or what would you want posted on your tombstone?

A powerful exercise to get at your sense of purpose is writing out your ideal tombstone epithet versus one that might be written about you if you spent your lifetime avoiding your core values.[5] For example, if you always avoided discomfort, your tombstone might say, 'Here lies Tom [or insert your own name

5 Harris, 2009.

here]. He never did anything that scared him.' Or, 'Here lies Sally. She was able to avoid any uncomfortable social situations.'

'Wow! This is a sobering and terrifying thought,' Celeste says.

Let's imagine now that you lived your life exactly the way that you would like. Let's imagine that you were able to find and honour your sense of purpose. Let's imagine that you were able to help and inspire countless people and that, twenty years from now, a film will be made about you. What would you want it to be about?

_____

_____

_____

_____

_____

_____

_____

_____

_____

_____

If this film does exactly what it is supposed to, how would you want it to inspire/affect others?

_____

_____

_____

_____

_____

4) Manage your regrets. As you are probably starting to realise, life is not meant to be about avoiding discomfort, it is meant to be about finding meaning. And this process is a bit of a balancing act. Sometimes, we might think that we are not avoiding anything when we are overly productive and over-achieving. After all, we are working hard every moment of every day. What could we possibly be avoiding?

Although hard work is most certainly a wonderful virtue, sometimes it can also become an escape mechanism. In over-working and overachieving, we are sometimes avoiding living our lives. Think of how often we might be giving up our time with friends or family members in order to work or make sure that we are able to tick off another item on our task list. And yet, at the end of their lives, no one has ever said, 'I wish I completed those items on my task list.'

Just like common avoidance (cancelling plans, avoiding giving talks, etc.), overwork can also be an avoidance of thoughts related to not being good enough, as well as past trauma and abuse. And although productivity is helpful with our mental and physical health, the lack of balance with our core values can lead to numerous regrets at the end of our lives.

A New Zealand palliative nurse, Bronnie Ware, who helped numerous people prepare for their transition to death, observed that most people who had regrets at the end of their lives essentially regretted not living a life according to their sense of purpose.

Here are the top five regrets of the dying according to Bronnie Ware:[6]

a.   I wish I hadn't worked so hard
b.   I wish I'd stayed in touch with my friends
c.   I wish I'd had the courage to express my true feelings
d.   I wish I'd had the courage to be myself, not what others expect of me
e.   I wish I had let myself be happier

'I think that one of my regrets would be about working too hard,' Hazeem says. 'I have not had a day off in over a year.'

'Wow,' Celeste says, 'I can see myself having all of these. The fourth one – the one about having the courage to be myself instead of what others expect of me – that one really got to me. I've spent years of my life trying to impress my birth family – my parents and my brother. I realise now that no matter what I do, they may never see me the way I want them to see me. And you know what? I am tired of living my life according to what other people expect of me. I have my wife; she is my family now. I have my friends; they are my chosen family. And I have you guys – my mental health family. I want to start living my life now, the way that I want to live it, and to allow myself to be happier.'

5) Treasure Chest Exercise. One way we can practise living a more meaningful life, with the fewest regrets possible, is

6 Warren, 2012.

through the Treasure Chest exercise, which allows us to evaluate our core values. Among the many monsters we already face, one of the most notable ones is the monster of our busy schedule. We might be so focused on one of our core values, such as work or education, that the other elements that we care about might fall by the wayside.

When I was in graduate school, a professor asked my classmates and me to track how we were spending our time week to week and notice how attentive we were to the different elements of our core values, such as learning, friendships, relationships, health, fun and others. I was mortified to learn that more than 95 per cent of my wakeful time was spent on school, the other 5 per cent on television and 0 per cent was spent with friends, family or on meaningful, enjoyable activities. This was a powerful wake-up call for me and I was determined to make a change. So, I began hosting weekly games nights with my friends and my partner, which allowed me to honour multiple core values at the same time.

Although life is essentially a balancing act of our core values, we can focus on being attentive to the different core values categories in order to help us to live a full life with few to no regrets.

We can think of core values as treasure chests. If we put too much gold into them, the treasure chests will overflow. And if we don't put much into them, the treasure chests will be only half full or near empty.

The illustration on page 150 shows a map of different core values treasure chests, each currently represented as 'empty'.

Take a look at these and consider where you currently are with your core values. Specifically, take a look at how much time and effort you are currently putting into each of these core values based on how much time and effort you would *ideally* like to put into this core value.

You can then draw the amount of gold coins that represents where you currently are in terms of meeting this core value (many coins would represent meeting this core value to a large degree). This decision would not be based on what your family, friends or society expect of you, but rather on your personal preference. For example, your family might place a strong emphasis on your getting a job right after school, whereas you might wish to go to university first, or vice versa. These are *your* core values, these are *your* treasures, not anyone else's, and only what you have to say and only how you feel matters.

As you are working on this exercise, keep in mind that the exact definitions of these core values are also up to your interpretation, no one else's. For instance, family could mean blood-related family, or it could mean chosen family. Some values might also overlap. Creativity and fandom might both include cosplay or writing fanfiction. For this exercise, identify your own definitions for each core value. Whatever these core values mean to you, the definitions for each are yours, and yours alone.

If you are perfectly happy with the amount of time and effort you are putting into your specific core value (such as friends), then you would draw the appropriate treasure chest as full of gold coins but not overflowing. If you think you are spending too much time on your career, for example, then that treasure chest would be overflowing. If you're not spending enough time on a particular core value, then that particular treasure chest would be less full accordingly, or even empty. Feel free to add your own treasure chests to this if there are any core values that aren't represented. Give it a try now.

'Wow, the visual was eye-opening,' Liz says. 'My career treasure chest is overflowing and most of the others are empty.'

'Most of mine are empty as well,' Shawn says. 'And none are full. I find that I want to do more in each of the important categories, but I haven't. I don't know if it was my anxiety or the reality of the current environment that has gotten in my way, but I know I definitely want to do more.'

6) Learning from your challenges. Everyone faces challenges and setbacks, even major superheroes like Batman, Iron Man and Captain Marvel. Facing challenges is not a failure, it is the core of resilience. Like a video game, every challenge you face has a steep learning curve, until you figure out how to face it and then level up. Once you level up, however, you are then likely to face another challenge, which you would then need to learn from as well. Every person and every superhero faces multiple challenges and it is not in spite of this fact but *because* of this fact that we look up to them. And you are a real-life superhero, one who has already faced multiple challenges and will continue to level up as you go.

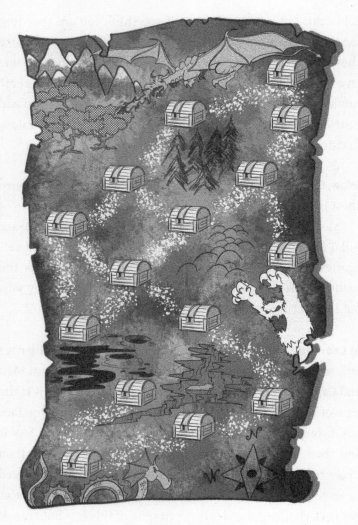

Fig. 10

In order to learn from our challenges, we need to devise an action plan and then test the results. Here are the steps that we can take:

a. Learning – heroes try to learn as much about the monster or the challenge that they are facing as possible in order to maximise their chances of overcoming it. This means that with each new challenge that we might face, such as anxiety, depression or a painful life event, we need to practise learning about how we experience it in our body and the kinds of thoughts that we are having about these events using our mindfulness, vulnerability and defusion skills.

b. Plan – heroes form a plan about how they will face a specific monster (e.g., through vulnerability and self-compassion skills) and also recruit sidekicks to help them. They also focus on the big picture – their sense of purpose and what the mission is for.

c. Carry out the plan – once the heroes form a plan, they try it out, even if they aren't sure if it will be successful, because they know that doing something is better than doing nothing. So, rather than avoiding taking any steps, see if there are any steps that you might be able to take in the direction of your plan to honour your sense of purpose.

d. Learn from the results – heroes rarely fully succeed on the first try. Instead, every time they try to face their monsters, they learn something. With time, the heroes

become less afraid of their monsters and learn ways to
face them.

e.   Form new plans – using the information from the initial plan, the heroes can create new plans to face their
monsters.

f.   Try again – the more the heroes learn about the monsters they are facing, the better they can learn to face
their monsters.

g.   Keep trying and never give up – remember your mission
as being a part of something that is very important to
you and also a part of something greater than yourself.
Never give up and keep superheroing.

'This is not going to be easy because I tend to be very hard on
myself,' Erika says. 'But I am going to try it out. In general, that
is more or less what I already do – formulate a plan and try it
out and adjust it as necessary, but I tend to judge myself very
harshly in the process. I am going to try it out from a gentler
perspective, if I can.'

'I am going to apply this approach to facing my anxiety,'
Celeste says. 'I am going to work towards leaving the house regularly and reducing my compulsions. I will work on a plan with
my wife and if we need to, we can always adjust the plan as
necessary.'

'I believe in you,' Liz says.

'Thanks, love.' Celeste smiles at her.

In fact, the best way to manage anxiety, especially OCD, is
through gradually facing your fears over time without engaging

in avoidance or compassion behaviours.[7] Remembering your sense of purpose and what you are doing it for can help you to stay on track with your plan.

7) Talk to your hero. When in doubt, you always have an option of talking to your hero. At any time, you can write out what you would want to say to your hero and then write out what your hero might say back to you.

'I really like this exercise,' Hazeem says. 'I know that it is imaginary, but it was also really meaningful for me to feel connected with my father again. Somehow, I feel a little less lonely and because of the exercise we did last time, I was able to reach out to my brother last week. We met up for a socially distanced walk and I got to meet my nephew for the first time. I have been having conversations with my father both in my mind and by writing to him over the past few days and have found that my spirits have been higher, and I am feeling more connected with other people as well.'

There is always much to learn and much to do. And it all starts with taking one step. Just one step. Are you ready?

---

7 Hezel & Simpson, 2019.

Chapter 7
Becoming a Superhero IRL

Have you ever heard of a phoenix? A phoenix is a magical bird, said to come from the sun, that goes through painful changes every once in a while. After the phoenix has gone through a painful change, it bursts into burning flames and then falls to ash. But then the phoenix rises again, stronger than before.

In fact, your internal pain, be it trauma, grief or anxiety, might make you feel like you are on fire. But like a phoenix, you will rise from the ashes, stronger than before. And this is your phoenix moment.

Fig. 11: Phoenix rising from the ashes.

The steps that you take to honour your sense of purpose are your hero steps, your rebirth, your post-traumatic growth, your actions to make this world a better place. This is when you become your very own version of a superhero in real life (IRL). So, with all the choices in the world to be the kind of hero that you want to be, where would you like to start?

One way to approach this question is to refer back to the treasure chest exercise from the previous chapter. Note which treasure chests were either empty or not as full as you would like them to be. This would imply that these core values are important to you, but they have not been addressed as much as you would like. For example, you might value your family (biological, relational or chosen family), but you might notice that you have been struggling with finding a way to spend more time with them. Of course, everyone experiences this. We all struggle with balancing out our values. Noticing the discrepancy between how much time and effort we would like to spend addressing each of our core values and how much time and effort we are actually able to put into each core value domain is never meant to be a shaming exercise. It is a simple fact of life that as we address one of our core value domains (for example, career or relationship), another domain might have less time dedicated to it (for example, friends or health). And so, without any shame, judgement or criticism, see if you can write down the main core value categories (the types of treasure chests) that were not as full as you personally would like them to be.

_____

_____

_____

_____

_____

Now, let's see if we can identify the hero steps that you can take to honour the core values that you wrote above. For example, in order to honour your friendships, you might elect to check in with your friends by phone once per week, have a virtual catch-up once per month, and send a supportive text twice per month (the exact details of these activities are up to you). Another example might be related to a core value of education. If this is a core value you'd like to address, you might, for example, want to make a list of universities you'd like to apply to, interview admissions counsellors, professors and students who already attend those universities, and then work on your applications.

For each core value you'd like to address, see if you can write down two to three hero steps that you would like to take at some point over the next year in order to honour that core value.

Core value: _____

Hero Steps: _____

_____

_____

Core value: _____

Hero Steps: _____

_____

_____

Core value: _____

Hero Steps: _____

_____

_____

Core value: _____

Hero Steps: _____

_____

_____

Core value: _____

Hero Steps: _____

_____

_____

Now, see if you would be willing to write down one or two hero steps from above as your commitment for this week. For example, you might write down that you would be willing to commit to texting one of your friends this week and exercising once for thirty seconds. Whatever your chosen hero steps are, they are exactly what you need to be doing. There are no steps that are too small because they all move you forward.

_____

_____

_____

Shawn sighs. 'I wrote that I would like to engage more with others. I was thinking of Batman. He helps people not only through fighting the villains but also by being there for his friends and supporting his sidekicks. I have always looked up to him. And I think I might have only been thinking about how I can help others in specific ways – firefighting and managing my contact with the virus. I guess there are other ways I can help, too. So, that's what my steps will be this week.'

'I really like that idea, Shawn,' Liz says. 'The idea of helping people in more than one way. I've always thought about helping people medically, but I can also help people through my education and experience. One of my unaddressed core values is giving women, especially women of colour, a voice. And so, for my steps, I would like to talk to my director about doing some kind of educational programmes at the hospital.'

'Well, I would like to work on my anxiety. I am tired of it holding me back,' Celeste says. 'I am working on creating steps to face my anxiety.'

Keep in mind that the steps you wrote out are your intentions, which means that they are not set in stone. Sometimes other more pressing hero steps might be important, and it is not only OK to be flexible in this process, it is necessary. It also means that we will inevitably have setbacks and difficulties along this journey and the idea is to continue to practise intention setting. A daily intention setting practice is the commitment to a small action or a way of being that you would like to focus on that day. For example, you can set an intention to focus on being more patient with others on a given day. Or, you might set an intention to reach out to your friend.

In order to practise intention setting, you can write down your intention on a piece of paper, your journal or on your electronic device and attempt to practise this intention throughout the day. At the end of the day, you can check in with yourself to see how your practice went. This check-in at the end of the day is never meant to be a shaming experience. Instead, the check-in is to see what went well and which obstacles arose for you that day (for example, a fight with your best friend that you could not possibly foresee).

You can then reset your intention the next day (whether it would be the same or a different intention from the day before) and continue to practise. As a friendly reminder, the key about an intention setting practice is that it is in fact a *practice*, which means that it is not meant to be perfect and there is no way of getting it wrong. The idea is just to try it out.

Let's try this exercise. First write down your intention for the day. Examples of daily intentions could include being more patient, being mindful, being kind, reaching out to friends, doing some work towards completing a project, spending some time cleaning, taking a few actions towards social justice, etc.

Please write down your intention for today:

_____

_____

_____

At the end of the day, please write out how this practice went. Be sure to refrain from shaming yourself. Write out what went well and any obstacles that came up for you, as well as how you might want to manage these obstacles should they arise again:

_____

_____

_____

_____

_____

You can continue this practice the next day and whenever possible, working through the hero steps that you have written out above, as well as adding new ones along the way.

'Ah, I have practised intention setting before,' Liz says, 'but the shaming part always got to me. I don't even think I was consciously doing it. The shame was just there. I will try being mindful of that when I practise this week.'

Another way to approach the question of how you would like to begin your superhero steps is to write out a list of all the actions you would like to take over the next year, for example, text a friend, apply to a university, spend time with a co-worker, go for a walk around the neighbourhood, etc. It could also include activities that at some point in your life made you feel good, such as reading, playing games, art or training your dog. These also count as superhero steps because they help you to power up and even help you to honour your self-care, hobbies and gaming core values.

After you write out the list of specific steps you would like to take, rank order them starting at one (being the easiest). For example, if you wrote down ten superhero steps, you would rank order them from one (one being the easiest action if you were to do it today) to ten (ten being the most challenging action if you were to do it today).

_____
_____
_____
_____
_____
_____
_____
_____
_____
_____
_____
_____

Once you have your list, you would start with the easiest item (if possible) and work on completing one (or more) item(s) per week. Think of this process as **levelling up.** Of course, each level that you complete will not be easy, but it will also be really rewarding.

'I really like seeing it presented in this way,' Celeste says. 'The list of steps as a way of levelling up, I can see how it can be like a game. A very hard game, for sure, but I'm willing to play. Here is the list I made:

1. Only washing my hands once whenever I wash them instead of continuously washing them until it feels 'right'.
2. Only scrubbing the packages once when they arrive.
3. Date nights.
4. Going for a walk around my block once per day.
5. Not asking my wife to wash her hands when I feel anxious, and instead just sitting with my anxiety.
6. Video hang-out with friends.
7. Going to the store.
8. Going for a walk in the park.
9. Driving more than ten miles from home.
10. Sitting with my anxiety when I feel uncertain.

'I actually started with the first step this past week even without knowing about this list. It was hard and I was certainly anxious, but I was able to do it. It felt really good to take this step.'

It makes sense that taking these steps will be uncomfortable and, at times, frightening. Success in this case does not equate to not being afraid. Success is showing up regardless of how you feel, even if you had to take a few detours. And if you can do that, then you have levelled up. Here are a few things to keep in mind to help you along the way:

1. Remember that the hardest part about taking superhero steps is the *anticipation* of doing it. In fact, 90 per cent of the time, your anxiety will be higher *before* you engage in any given step than *while* you are actually engaging in it. Remind yourself that you are most likely going to feel better once you actually start engaging in the task compared to when you are waiting to start it. This is actually why procrastination tends to heighten people's anxiety – we stay in the anticipatory stage longer when we are procrastinating, which usually heightens our anxiety and reduces our self-confidence. However, once you start a particular superhero step, it will usually be easier to continue and subsequently finish the task, allowing you to level up.

2. Remember the big picture: what it is all for. When you are starting to doubt yourself and your abilities, when you feel the pull of avoidance and procrastination, remind yourself of your sense of purpose. Remind yourself of the kind of hero that you want to be, remind yourself of what your hero would say to you. Remind yourself that it might be challenging but it will also be worth it in the end.

3. Imagine the consequences of never taking these steps. Imagine what might happen if you never reach out to

your friends or never take a chance to work on your dream project. Remember the regrets that you might have at the end of your life and remind yourself of your life goals.

4. Imagine yourself succeeding. Imagine that you can take these steps and imagine that, over time, things will go your way. Imagine what it would be like to complete these steps and the steps that follow them. What would that be like? What would your life look like if you were able to do everything on your list? What would you look forward to and what would you be most excited about?

5. Recruit sidekicks. If possible, see if you can recruit a sidekick (or two), someone who can encourage you and support you. This could be a friend, a family member, a neighbour, an internet friend, a therapist, or someone else you would be able to recruit. Most superheroes have sidekicks. Some people struggle to ask for additional support in this way. However, having sidekicks is not a weakness; it can provide you with a pool of inner strength and help you to better manage any obstacles and setbacks you might face.

6. Speaking of setbacks, it is crucial to allow for them. In any activity, in any sport, in any video game or board game, setbacks happen. This means that we might set an intention to try one of these activities but then struggle to start, face an unexpected obstacle that might prevent us from starting, or start but be unable

to complete the intended task. This is perfectly OK and completely normal. Every single human in the universe goes through experiences like these. Setbacks are not a failure. They are obstacles. They might initially slow you down or get in your way, but ultimately, facing your obstacles is how you can learn and grow. So, when (not if but when) you are inevitably facing an obstacle, whether it is your anxiety about starting it, your schedule or another unexpected situation, recognise and name this experience. Remind yourself, 'I am facing an obstacle right now. Every superhero faces obstacles on a regular basis. It makes sense that this would be challenging for me right now. And because this task is very important to me, I am going to keep trying and trying until I complete it.'

The following worksheet can help you to track and address some of the setbacks you might face:

Worksheet: Facing Setbacks

Everyone faces setbacks from time to time. A setback refers to an interruption of someone's progress. For example, when Wonder Woman plans to help innocent civilians during the First World War, she might experience a setback when one of her plans doesn't go as she might have hoped.

Although all heroes face obstacles, it does not mean that all hope is lost. Instead, it might mean that the hero will need to use some of their skills (such as a magic lasso, magical skills,

Spidey senses or other abilities) and possibly ask their fellow heroes for support as well.

Even after you have completed your Superhero Therapy training, there will be times when your old monsters show up again and new ones might arise. Remember: a return of the old problems does not mean that you are back 'at square one'. In fact, you can't be because you have changed. You have learned many skills and, as a result, you are not the same person you used to be. For example, Harry Potter might encounter a complicated spell or potion that he has not experienced before, or he might face a return of his old symptoms (headaches or painful memories), but it does not mean that he has unlearned magic. He can still use the spells and tools he has at his disposal and ask his friends and mentors for help too.

In order to help you during those unpredictable setbacks, let's list all the skills you have learned, especially the ones you have found to be helpful during your Superhero Therapy training.

You can write them out:

_____

_____

_____

_____

_____

_____

_____

_____

_____

_____

Now that you've identified your emergency skills, let's also identify the big picture. For example, Batman's sense of purpose is
helping people and making Gotham City safer for everyone.
What is your sense of purpose? What is it all for? Please write
out your answer:

_____

_____

_____

_____

_____

_____

_____

_____

_____

Finally, please write out your inner strengths. Oftentimes, we
might forget how resilient we actually are, how kind we are
and how much we have already overcome. Please write or draw
your greatest strengths below and write out one or two sentences of encouragement for yourself, such as 'I believe in you',
'You matter' or 'You make a difference'.

1. Hero up! See if you can embody your hero. Perhaps take a posture that your hero would take when facing a challenge like this or when preparing to complete a task, such as the one you are facing right now. Sit or stand the way that your hero would. Notice the position of your shoulders, whether you are looking up or looking down, whether you are clenching your jaw and tensing your forehead, or whether these areas are relaxed. Take a moment and sit or stand with your arms at your sides, like Superman or Wonder Woman. This posture has been shown to help people feel more confident when they are facing anxiety-provoking situations, such as public speaking or interviews.[1] Similarly, wearing a symbol that represents a beloved hero, like Batman or Wonder Woman, can also help us to remain on task for longer periods of time compared to how we might function without these symbols.[2] For example, wearing

1 Cuddy, et al., 2012.
2 White & Carlson, 2015.

a Batman keychain or a Wonder Woman bracelet might help you to feel more willing and more courageous to participate in a particular task and might make it easier for you to maintain your attention on this task over a longer period of time.

2. When in doubt, move around. Movement researcher Kelly McGonigal finds that movement can boost our mood and can help us better manage our stress and anxiety.[3] She also adds that dancing and bouncing around can be especially helpful for boosting our mood, as it can boost our endorphin levels (our body's 'feel good' chemicals). So, if you are feeling blue, turn on some music and dance around, even if you are sitting down to do it. Just bouncing to music while sitting down for at least five minutes can be helpful. Alternatively, you can dance or bounce around while doing your chores or when engaging in some of the superhero tasks you listed above.

A few years ago, I was working with a client who had a phobia of driving. Her boyfriend would normally drive her to sessions and drop her off. My client, let's call her 'Casey', was also a big *Harry Potter* fan. She stated that the series of films helped her to have the courage to face her own anxieties and phobias as well.

I will never forget the day that we went on a drive together. Casey was wearing her Gryffindor scarf; she turned the ignition and started the car.

3 McGonigal, 2019.

'How are you feeling?' I asked her.

'So scared,' she said. 'But I'm ready.'

With that, Casey turned on the music and pulled out of the driveway. She bounced around to the music as we slowly drove around the block. She was shaking from anxiety but used her dancing as a way to go with her anxiety rather than to try to suppress it. When we drove around the block and parked, she was smiling and crying at the same time.

'I did it!'

To this day, my heart warms when I think of her courage and the way she was willing to meet her biggest fear with a symbol of her favourite fandom and with a little bit of dance. Casey now drives by herself and although she still feels nervous from time to time, she doesn't let her anxiety hold her back any longer.

'Yes!' Celeste says. 'That's what I need to do with my anxiety. I am going to put on my Wonder Woman shirt and go for a long walk today.'

The key with any new exercise is to practise it regularly. After you've been doing something for over three weeks, it becomes a habit and it is easier to maintain. You will undoubtedly run into challenges along the way, so see what you can learn from them. Treat challenges as your teachers, your guides to help you move forward. And in case of an emergency, if you are hit with an obstacle so big that it seems impossible that you will get over it, remember your skills – remember your mindfulness practices, your vulnerability armour and your self-compassion potion. Remember your sense of purpose, remember what you stand for, and remember the heroes that can guide you and the sidekicks that can support you through it. It is always OK to slow down, to take a little break, in order to then rise up like the phoenix that you are and get right back on your heroic path.

Two weeks later

'Hello.' Erika smiles. 'So . . . I did it! I asked my work for a week off for a staycation. I have never taken time off that was not related to travel, but going away is not so easy right now, and I need the break just as badly. But I actually felt kind of guilty asking for it. At first, the clinic director was trying to give me a hard time about it. He said that they are short staffed and it's not a good time to take time off. I started to feel very guilty and almost told him that I had changed my mind. And as I was about to tell him that I won't be taking my vacation time, I felt dizzy and very anxious. And frustrated. And I realised that I have been trying to take a sick day, or just a day to myself, for almost a year but it is never a good time for me to do so. I realised that if I keep waiting for it to be a good time, I will never have any time off.

'I also thought about what we talked about in terms of self-compassion being an investment into our resilience and healing. I realised that being burned out made it challenging for me to see my patients. I remembered the study you mentioned that showed that burnout can contribute to medical mistakes and I realised that my core values were basically in competition with one another. On the one hand, I value helping people;

this includes both my patients and my co-workers. On the other hand, I also value being thorough and prepared, which I usually am anyway, but I need my rest to be able to keep doing as much work as I am doing. Then I also thought about my core value of spending time with my family and I realised that I had not had a full day with my husband and kids in over a year. We are always either working or helping someone else, all of which is important to me, but so is time with my family.

'So, I ended up stating that I need to take a week off and gave the clinic director the choices for my preferred days off. He actually honoured my first choice and gave me the following week off, which was last week. I spent the week with my family, just catching up on rest, games, puzzles and cuddles. It was wonderful.'

'How wonderful!' Hazeem says, smiling. 'I am so glad that you were able to spend time with those you love. I was able to do that also. I saw my brother a few more times. We went for a walk and talked about our father a lot. It was the closest I have felt to my brother in a long time.

'And then, something wonderful happened. I was at work and Amir, my friend, came into the store. He is the one that was teaching me sign language. I was so happy to see him. I ran up to him and started signing to ask him how he was doing and telling him that I had been thinking about him and hoping that he was all right. He just stood there, surprised. He didn't know that I had been studying on my own to be able to talk to him. He just kept signing, "Thank you. Thank you." He had tears in his eyes. We both did.

'He has been coming to the store every day since then. He told me that he had been feeling very depressed, and so he had stayed home. He said that he was lonely but feeling too depressed to leave the house. We have been talking, and well, yesterday we decided that we should be roommates. He doesn't have anyone and doesn't have much money, and I work many hours, and I need someone to take care of my cat, Marshmallow. So, he is moving in this weekend. I have never before lived with a friend, but I am very excited.

'And there is one more thing. Last night, my father came to me in my dream. He said that he was proud of me for helping a friend. He hugged me and he said that he is always alive in my heart and in my actions. When I woke up, I felt like he was still standing with me, by my side. It was as if the sun rose again after a dark night. And I am so grateful.'

'Wow, Hazeem!' Liz smiles at him. 'I wish I could give you a hug right now. That's wonderful, and just made my day!'

'Ah, thank you, my friend.' Hazeem smiles at her. 'I hope you have been well?'

'I have, actually, thank you so much for asking.' Her smile widens. 'I talked to the hospital director about my idea of providing some kind of an ongoing education to the staff about women and minority patients, and the director was thrilled about it. She told me that she fully supports my idea and we are working towards launching several courses that I will be teaching virtually to the hospital staff. We also talked about starting a diversity club at the hospital and yesterday, we had our first meeting. I expected two, maybe three people. Well, twenty-eight people showed up to this online meeting. They voted for me to be the president of the club and we are going to have bi-monthly meetings. I also started a weekly virtual peer mental health support group for healthcare providers, just for all of us to talk about what we are going through and support one another. We start next week. I have been getting multiple messages over the past week telling me how grateful people are about both of these groups and how meaningful it is for them to have this outlet. I am so excited! I have more energy than I've had in a long time and I'm thrilled and deeply grateful to be doing the work that I do. I even made a fun video for my co-workers sharing our memories of hanging out together, dancing around at the office, as well as pictures of our fun group chats. My co-workers loved it and I felt much more connected to them than I had in a long time. So overall, I felt both grateful and empowered over the past couple of weeks.'

'That's incredible. Congratulations, Liz. Congratulations to all of you,' Shawn says. 'As always, I don't think of my actions as necessarily worth mentioning but I recognise that it could be my internal self-critic talking. So, here I am, putting on my armour of vulnerability. Phew . . . OK.' He takes a few breaths. 'Over the past couple of weeks I would only allow myself a short amount of time to wipe my station. I kept in mind that my anxiety is likely going to remain high whether or not I am wiping and cleansing, so I focused on only cleaning as much as the guidelines suggest we should.

'Then I started talking to another firefighter at the station, Jake. I asked him how he was doing, and at first he just said, "Fine." Somehow, we got talking, and I ended up opening up to him about my anxiety, about mental health in general, about how 9/11 affected me, and about this group. You have to remember that firefighters don't often talk about this stuff, so it was very hard. But then he started sharing. He actually broke down and said that he'd been feeling very depressed and alone. He shared that he has panic attacks sometimes and has never talked to anyone about this. I told him that therapy can be helpful, and he said he will look into it.

'I realised that in my efforts to keep everyone safe, I also pushed everyone away. So, over the past few weeks I started chatting to more of my guys at the station, and last Saturday we actually tossed the ball around to one another. We kept our distance and were wearing masks, but it was nice to do that. I also spent time with my wife and kids. We went to the beach, we read together, we meditated together, it was really nice. I want my kids to know that it's OK to feel anxious and that they can learn ways to manage their anxiety. And then yesterday at work, one of my guys called me Batman for some reason. I am not really sure what made him say it, but it just hit me right in the heart. It was one of those savouring moments, you know?'

How about you? Would you be willing to share your experiences of taking any kind of superhero steps? Either your victories or your setbacks? Anything you'd be willing to share?

_____

_____

_____

_____

_____

_____

_____

_____

_____

'I always love it when you share. It empowers me. So, thank you,' Celeste says to you. 'The past two weeks have been both challenging and exciting at the same time. I set my intention to work on my superhero step list, targeting one item per week, starting from the one I rated as "easiest". The first item on my list was to only wash my hands once instead of continuously washing them until it feels "right". At first, when I washed my hands after handling a delivery package, I wanted to keep washing and washing. But I stopped after the one time. My anxiety went way, way up. I was shaky and my heart was pounding. I practised the "Taking the dog off the leash" exercise and just sat back and allowed my emotions to "run around". At first, it got worse, but over time, my emotions settled. It took a while, but I just sat back and observed them in my body. By the time my emotions settled, I felt exhausted but exhilarated too.

'After a few days, this process got easier and I decided to try the second item on my list, only scrubbing the packages once when they arrive. I followed the same process as I did with reducing my hand washing. At first my anxiety went back up again, but it reduced faster than when I started working on reducing hand washing. I'm still working on this one, but I also decided to try having a date night with my wife, which was item number three on my list and I decided to combine it with my number four, which was to go for a walk around the block. Now, I have left the house a few times since the pandemic started but I don't do it often. So, when I suggested it to Julie, she was practically in tears. We dressed up like we used to on our date nights and walked around the block a few times.

'When we came home, I was so thrilled and then I realised that there are probably other people who haven't left the house very much. I posted on a local app asking neighbours if anyone needed a walking buddy. A few people responded and a few others stated that they were unable to go for walks but could use some help getting groceries. So, over the past week, I have been going for walks for at least fifteen minutes every day, either with Julie or with one of my neighbours, and getting groceries for people who need them. I also started sharing posts on social media about mental health to support other people who are having a hard time. I still get anxious, but I have been using it as energy fuel to power up and take the actions that I want to take.'

Fig. 12: Celeste being a superhero.

You might recall some time ago, we discussed four types of trauma response – fight, flight, freeze and fawn.[4] Well, I would like to add a fifth response to this mix – **Empower!** This response is your ability to grow after your experiences, to make meaning out of what happened to you, and to use your knowledge and skills to then help other people. You are here for a reason. You have a mission and your work here is only beginning. You are meant to help the world and you have already been making this world a better place. You might not ever fully know the extent of how many lives you have touched but know this: because of you, there are people who are alive today. Because of you, someone felt more hopeful in their darkest moment. Because of you, someone knows that they are not alone.

So, from the bottom of my heart, thank you for being wonderful.

4 Walker, 2013.

Chapter 8
Your Survivor Story

Your origin story might be the very beginning of your heroic journey, but it doesn't define who you are. Your actions do. And your core values do. And today, we are going to work on combining your origin story with what you have learned along the way, and with your heroic actions. This is essentially your origin story from an empowerment perspective. For example, many superheroes have a tragic origin story in which they lose a loved one or go through another kind of trauma. This event in some instances can become the catalyst in the hero's future choices, often inspiring them to become a protector, ensuring that others don't suffer the same fate they did. Batman is a powerful example of this kind of survivor story.

Traumatic origin stories are not necessary to unleash our heroic potential but for some individuals, going through a traumatic event can make them more empathic and passionate about helping others who are going through the same situation.

'I was reflecting on my survivor story,' Erika says. 'I think that my origin story actually starts with my childhood. My family and I came to the United States as immigrants. My life hasn't been easy, but it has been good. I had to work very hard for everything. I worked hard to get into a good college, a good medical school, to become the kind of doctor that I wanted to be. It was a challenging but also a powerful journey for me. I think somewhere along the way, I became so focused on work, that I forgot that I am a human, too; that just like my patients, I deserve care and compassion, too.

'This pandemic pushed me and rattled me. It showed me how far I'll go to help my patients and it also showed me how important my own self-care is, that is, if I want to be able to maintain the same level of hard work. I never realised that self-care is an investment in our healing and empowerment. And over the past few weeks, I have been able to see and feel it for myself. I still feel anxious at times, but I find that now my anxiety is much more manageable, and if anything, it is helping me to stay focused on my work and my family. I have always talked to my patients about self-care, but this is the first time I was able to really practise it myself to this extent.

'Being a woman of colour and an immigrant, I was used to my choices being questioned; so used to it, in fact, that it became almost the status quo. But this pandemic unleashed something in me. I would not allow myself to become complacent and I do not want my colleagues to become complacent either. I started having conversations with my colleagues about the latest research articles I'm finding and also about how we are treating one another. Your work, Liz, really inspired me to start these conversations as well. There is still a lot I would like to continue to work on in terms of my well-being and burnout prevention, but recognising the effects of burnout and the crucial significance of self-care was very important to me.'

'Thanks, Erika.' Liz smiles at her. 'I really appreciate that and appreciate what you are doing. For me, when I was thinking about my survivor story, I realised that like Erika, my origin story began long before the pandemic. I think it began when my nana died. Realising the injustices she faced from the medical system made me want to make a difference. I was barely an adult when 9/11 happened and this tragedy reinforced my decision to go into healthcare, as did Hurricane Katrina.

'I realised that the way I respond to tragedies is that I need to be able to contribute in some way, otherwise, I feel helpless and devastated. I don't think helping is just my coping mechanism. I think that helping is my superpower. And so, taking action by creating the educational courses on treating women and treating people of colour is helping me to get back to my hero's journey of helping others, as well as advocating for others.

'I realised too that if I feel a certain way, chances are that other people feel that way as well, and so a large part of my survivor's journey now focuses on mental health advocacy and reaching out to others. I felt incredibly alone for months and now I realise that countless others feel the same way. Every time I feel lonely and depressed, I reach out to someone else to check on them or post something about mental health on social media, following your example, Celeste. And although I would not say that I don't face my monsters any longer – I do – I have found that I don't have to face them alone, and I can use my voice and my experience to help other people feel seen, heard and supported too.'

Fig. 13: Superhero Liz teaching.

'Like Batman.' Shawn smiles at her.

'Like Batman.' Liz smiles.

'I guess I can go next,' Shawn says. 'I suppose my origin story began on 9/11 but my survivor story began that day, too. I saw a horrific tragedy and act of terrorism, and many, many deaths. But what I also saw was kindness: this pure, all-encompassing kindness in everyone in all of New York. I saw the power of compassion that day, that week, that year. I saw that kindness can help people heal even as they are still hurting. I saw that connection can help people to feel more empowered in life's most crucial moments. And after that day, I knew that I wanted to always be prepared for a disaster, to be able to help people and also offer the type of kindness that I saw being so crucial to people's well-being.

'I have a wife that I love, and two wonderful children. I love my friends and I love my job and my fellow firefighters. I also have a lot to lose and that makes me feel vulnerable, and sometimes afraid, not for me, for them. At first, I was ashamed to talk about how much anxiety I was going through. But then it made sense to me. I was anxious because I care. I learned that the inverse of my anxiety points to my sense of purpose. And then I stopped fighting the anxiety. I embraced it just like I embrace my children. And something in me soothed just then.

'Like Liz, I realised that if I am anxious, then other people might be going through a hard time too, people with loved ones who are living with cancer, people with loved ones with risk factors, and people who are pregnant or whose partners are pregnant. At first, I stayed away from everyone, trying to protect them, trying to protect my family, and other people we might come in contact with. But, over time, I saw that being there for other people and helping people is something that is most meaningful to me. I realised that there are different ways to help and I realised that I have the ability to help others around me.

'I am still learning. I am still growing. I am grateful for what I have and for what I have been privileged enough to contribute. And when in doubt, I can certainly ask Batman for guidance.'

If you are willing, please share your survivor story with the group. Feel free to write it down either below or on a separate sheet of paper. Please don't worry about grammar, punctuation or your handwriting for this exercise.

_____

_____

_____

_____

_____

_____

_____

_____

_____

'Aww, that was so lovely, you guys!' Celeste says. 'I am very honoured to have gotten to know all five of you. Like some of you, I initially thought that my origin story began with the pandemic. But I see now that it actually started a long time ago, in my childhood. Growing up in a home in which my every action was criticised and my brother's every step was celebrated, being discouraged from being myself and scolded for every decision I made, caused me to be indecisive and anxious.

'Long before the pandemic, I struggled with making decisions, and I was often unable to fall asleep with worry about just about everything. Uncertainty would make me panic, often making me feel unsafe. When the pandemic started, I would do anything possible to feel safe again, which started out as hand washing, wiping surfaces and wiping packages. Then it transferred to other compulsions, like counting everything, having to drink from certain glasses but not others, wearing certain clothes but not others, and other rules my mind would make up to try to create a sense of control and safety. After a while, going outside became impossible because everything was terrifying – stepping outside, stepping on cracks in the pavement, not stepping on cracks in the pavement, touching trees and lamp-posts, or not touching them. No matter what I did, my anxiety monster was screaming at me that I was doing something wrong and that I would get punished for doing it wrong by something bad happening to me or someone I love.

'However, over time, I learned to be mindful of my anxiety, I learned to sit with it, and I learned to have compassion for it. I learned that my history of child abuse likely caused me to not trust myself and my decisions. By honouring my sense of purpose of being connected with my wife and my friends, I was able to find the courage that I needed to face my fears.

'I also realised that, like the rest of you, I care about helping people. Since I am not in the healthcare field and I am not a first responder, I initially wasn't sure how I could contribute. But then I realised that just like me, countless other people are probably struggling with anxiety as well. By starting the neighbourhood walking group, I was able to meet other neighbours who were feeling lonely and was able to coordinate care, such as grocery shopping for people who were unable to go to the supermarket. We are now helping seven households with groceries and I am coordinating twelve volunteers. I have been going out every single day for the past month. I realise that my anxiety might not ever completely go away, but, interestingly, I've noticed that the more hero steps I take, despite how I feel, the less overwhelmed I feel by anxiety. I still don't feel "at ease" but the end result of all these actions tends to be worth whatever discomfort I might have felt. I plan to continue to create new hero steps when I am done with my list and continue to honour my sense of purpose. And from the bottom of my heart, thank you all so much for being on this journey with me.'

'Thank you so much, Celeste. Thank you all, my friends,' Hazeem says. 'This journey with all of you has been a truly magical one for me. For me, the Kashmir earthquake was my origin story, as was the loss of my father during the COVID pandemic. Never in my life had I ever felt so much pain and anguish. And I do not think that I fully allowed myself to grieve his death before this group. I think that I was afraid of facing the pain of his loss; I thought it would kill me. However, facing it, I found relief. I still miss my father every day, but I also feel closer to him and to my brother now. I feel more like myself again. I feel happier and having a roommate has been a wonderful change as well. I am working on living my life according to my sense of purpose and with as few regrets as possible. I am practising my intention setting every morning before work and my mindfulness exercises in the evenings. I just wanted to say thank you to all five of you for going on this journey with me. I am forever grateful.'

As with any sport or any skill, practising allows us to maintain our progress. When times are challenging, it might be hard to remember the skills that we have learned and the allies that we have made along the way. That's why we are going to create an emotional safety plan for how to approach old problems and new obstacles when they arise. It might be helpful to have a copy of this list in your wallet or a photo of it in your phone.

First, please list some of the previous challenges you've struggled with, whether or not you continue to experience them today. For example, depression, anxiety and other concerns:

_____

_____

_____

_____

_____

Next, please write out or draw some of the symptoms that you might need to look out for, some signs that you might be facing these monsters again. For example, you might notice that you are feeling irritable or not wanting to be around people, that you have a stomach-ache or headache or feel more sad or anxious than usual.

Next, let's think about which skills you can use to help you support yourself and find a sense of emotional safety if you are faced with these obstacles again. For example, you might wish to go into your Batcave for some time or have an imaginary (or real) conversation with your mentor. Please write out some examples of skills you can readily use if these problems were to arise again, as well as everything you'd like to be able to remember and hold on to, specific insights, quotes or practices.

_____
_____
_____
_____
_____
_____
_____
_____
_____

Finally, please write out an emergency number that you can call or text if you are having a rough time, for example, a crisis number (for calling or texting), your therapist's number, or the number of your best friend who would be able to be there for you:

_____
_____
_____
_____
_____

As we are coming to a close, remember to make some time to review the skills you find helpful from time to time. It can be helpful to schedule some time on a weekly basis to review your skills for fifteen to twenty minutes, for example. Another way to maintain your progress is to turn it into a game. Here is one way to do it:

Gamify Your Progress

One fun way you can practise your Superhero Therapy training skills is by making them into a game. The game rules are simple: once per week (or more frequently, if you'd like), you are invited to spend fifteen minutes reviewing and practising one of the skills you learned as part of Superhero Therapy. Every time you complete a practice, you earn one point. Every ten points earned allow you to level up in this game, earning you a small prize. Completing five levels allows you to earn a big prize.

In order to play this game, you would need an ally. This could be a family member, a partner or a friend who can help you to remember to practise and to decide which prizes you would get for completing your levels.

Write out the name of your ally: _____

Write out an idea for a small prize you'd like to earn for completing ten points: _____

_____

Write out an idea for a large prize you'd like to earn for completing five levels: _____

_____

As you and your ally play the game, you can use the table below to keep track of your points:

In this world, all seven billion of us have a role to play. It is up to us to take action; it is up to us to advocate for the kind of change we would like to see in the world. And it is up to us to band together and do our part to make this world a better place. Each person's way of helping might be different from another's and this is a wonderful thing. We each have a role to play and everything that you do helps. You are helping. You make a difference. And this here is your journey. You are the hero of this story. And you are the Chosen One. Keep super-heroing, and don't forget your cape.

Date	Skill(s) Completed	Point(s) earned	Current Level	Prize after completing this level	Prize after completing 5 levels
Level Up	Small Prize Earned	Great Job!	Keep Going!		

References

Ahola, K., Väänänen, A., Koskinen, A., Kouvonen, A. & Shirom, A. (2010). Burnout as a predictor of all-cause mortality among industrial employees: a 10-year prospective register-linkage study. *Journal of Psychosomatic Research, 69*(1), 51–7.

Arletti, R. & Bertolini, A. (1987). Oxytocin acts as an antidepressant in two animal models of depression. *Life Sciences, 41*(14), 1725–30.

Bellosta-Batalla, M., Blanco-Gandía, M. C., Rodríguez-Arias, M., Cebolla, A., Pérez-Blasco, J. & Moya-Albiol, L. (2020). Increased salivary oxytocin and empathy in students of clinical and health psychology after a mindfulness and compassion-based intervention. *Mindfulness*, 1–12.

Berrol, C. F. (2006). Neuroscience meets dance/movement therapy: Mirror neurons, the therapeutic process and empathy. *The Arts in Psychotherapy, 33*(4), 302–15.

Boden, M. T., Bernstein, A., Walser, R. D., Bui, L., Alvarez, J. & Bonn-Miller, M. O. (2012). Changes in facets of mindfulness and posttraumatic stress disorder treatment outcome. *Psychiatry Research, 200*(2–3), 609–13.

Brown, B. (2007). *I Thought It Was Just Me: Women reclaiming power and courage in a culture of shame.* Gotham Books.

Brown, B. (2010). *The Gifts of Imperfection: Let go of who you think you're supposed to be and embrace who you are.* Hazelden Publishing.

Brown, B. (2015). *Daring Greatly: How the courage to be vulnerable transforms the way we live, love, parent, and lead.* New York, NY: Penguin.

Cacioppo, J. T., Fowler, J. H. & Christakis, N. A. (2009). Alone in the crowd: the structure and spread of loneliness in a large social network. *Journal of Personality and Social Psychology, 97*(6), 977.

Crespi, B. J. (2016). Oxytocin, testosterone, and human social cognition. *Biological Reviews, 91*(2), 390–408.

Cuddy, A. J., Wilmuth, C. A. & Carney, D. R. (2012). The benefit of power posing before a high-stakes social evaluation. *Harvard Business School Working Paper, No. 13-027,* http://nrs.harvard.edu/urn-3:HUL.InstRepos:9547823

Culp, B. (Director). (2017). *Look to the Sky* [Documentary]. United States.

Dowling, T. (2018). Compassion does not fatigue! *The Canadian Veterinary Journal, 59*(7), 749–50.

Dyrbye, L. N., Thomas, M. R., Massie, F. S., Power, D. V., Eacker, A., Harper, W., ... & Sloan, J. A. (2008). Burnout and suicidal ideation among US medical students. *Annals of Internal Medicine, 149*(5), 334–41.

References

Epel, E. S. & Lithgow, G. J. (2014). Stress biology and aging mechanisms: toward understanding the deep connection between adaptation to stress and longevity. *Journals of Gerontology Series A: Biomedical Sciences and Medical Sciences, 69*(Suppl_1), S10–S16.

Felitti, V. J., Anda, R. F., Nordenberg, D. & Williamson, D. F. (1998). Adverse childhood experiences and health outcomes in adults: The Ace study. *Journal of Family and Consumer Sciences, 90*(3), 31.

Flanagan, J. C., Sippel, L. M., Wahlquist, A., Moran-Santa Maria, M. M. & Back, S. E. (2018). Augmenting prolonged exposure therapy for PTSD with intranasal oxytocin: a randomized, placebo-controlled pilot trial. *Journal of Psychiatric Research, 98*, 64–9.

Friedmann, E., Thomas, S. A., Liu, F., Morton, P. G., Chapa, D., Gottlieb, S. S. & Sudden Cardiac Death in Heart Failure Trial (SCD-HeFT) Investigators (2006). Relationship of depression, anxiety, and social isolation to chronic heart failure outpatient mortality. *American Heart Journal, 152*(5), 940–e1.

Frijling, J. L. (2017). Preventing PTSD with oxytocin: effects of oxytocin administration on fear neurocircuitry and PTSD symptom development in recently trauma-exposed individuals. *European Journal of Psychotraumatology, 8*(1), 1302652.

Grillon, C., Krimsky, M., Charney, D. R., Vytal, K., Ernst, M. & Cornwell, B. (2013). Oxytocin increases anxiety to unpredictable threat. *Molecular Psychiatry, 18*(9), 958–60.

Hagenmuller, F., Rössler, W., Wittwer, A. & Haker, H. (2014). Juicy lemons for measuring basic empathic resonance. *Psychiatry Research, 219*(2), 391–6.

Harris, R. (2009). *ACT Made Simple: An Easy-To-Read Primer on Acceptance and Commitment Therapy.* Oakland, CA: New Harbinger.

Hayes, S. C. (2019). *A Liberated Mind: How to pivot toward what matters.* New York, NY: Avery.

Hezel, D. M. & Simpson, H. B. (2019). Exposure and response prevention for obsessive-compulsive disorder: A review and new directions. *Indian Journal of Psychiatry, 61*(Suppl 1), S85–S92.

Higa, K. T., Mori, E., Viana, F. F., Morris, M. & Michelini, L. C. (2002). Baroreflex control of heart rate by oxytocin in the solitary-vagal complex. *American Journal of Physiology-Regulatory, Integrative and Comparative Physiology, 282*(2), R537–45.

Kemp, A. H., Quintana, D. S., Kuhnert, R. L., Griffiths, K., Hickie, I. B. & Guastella, A. J. (2012). Oxytocin increases heart rate variability in humans at rest: implications for social approach-related motivation and capacity for social engagement. *PloS One, 7*(8), e44014.

King, A. P., Block, S. R., Sripada, R. K., Rauch, S., Giardino, N., Favorite, T., ... & Liberzon, I. (2016). Altered default mode network (DMN) resting state functional connectivity following a mindfulness-based exposure therapy for posttraumatic stress disorder (PTSD) in combat veterans of Afghanistan and Iraq. *Depression and Anxiety, 33*(4), 289–99.

Klimecki, O. & Singer, T. (2012). Empathic distress fatigue rather than compassion fatigue? Integrating findings from empathy research in psychology and social neuroscience. In B. Oakley, A. Knafo, G. Madhavan & D. S. Wilson (Eds.). *Pathological Altruism,* 368–83. New York, NY: Oxford University Press.

LePera, N. (2011). Relationships between boredom proneness, mindfulness, anxiety, depression, and substance use. *The New School Psychology Bulletin, 8*(2), 15–25.

Martins, D., Davies, C., De Micheli, A., Oliver, D., Krawczun-Rygmaczewska, A., Fusar-Poli, P. & Paloyelis, Y. (2020). Intranasal oxytocin increases heart-rate variability in men at clinical high risk for psychosis: a proof-of-concept study. *Translational Psychiatry, 10*(1), 1–12.

McCracken, L. M. & Vowles, K. E. (2014). Acceptance and commitment therapy and mindfulness for chronic pain: Model, process, and progress. *American Psychologist, 69*(2), 178.

McGonigal, K. (2019). *The Joy of Movement: How exercise helps us find happiness, hope, connection, and courage.* New York, NY: Penguin.

Morina, N. (2011). Rumination and avoidance as predictors of prolonged grief, depression, and posttraumatic stress in female widowed survivors of war. *The Journal of Nervous and Mental Disease, 199*(12), 921–7.

Neff, K. (2004). Self-compassion and psychological well-being. *Constructivism in the Human Sciences, 9*(2), 27–38.

Neff, K. (2011). *Self-compassion: The proven power of being kind to yourself.* New York, NY: Harper Collins.

Neff, K. D. & Dahm, K. A. (2015). Self-compassion: What it is, what it does, and how it relates to mindfulness. In *Handbook of mindfulness and self-regulation* (pp. 121–37). Springer, New York, NY.

Neff, K. & Germer, C. (2018). *The Mindful Self-Compassion Workbook: A proven way to accept yourself, build inner strength, and thrive.* Guilford Publications.

Papazoglou, K. & Chopko, B. (2017). The role of moral suffering (moral distress and moral injury) in police compassion fatigue and PTSD: An unexplored topic. *Frontiers in Psychology, 8.*

Polack, E. (2018). *New Cigna study reveals loneliness at epidemic levels in America. Cigna,* 1.

Price, J. (2013). Explaining human conflict: Human needs theory and the insight approach. In *Conflict Resolution and Human Needs* (pp. 126–41). Routledge.

Resick, P. A. & Schnicke, M. K. (1992). Cognitive processing therapy for sexual assault victims. *Journal of Consulting and Clinical Psychology, 60*(5), 748.

Ringenbach, R. T. (2009). A comparison between counsellors who practice meditation and those who do not on compassion fatigue, compassion satisfaction, burnout and self-compassion (Doctoral dissertation, University of Akron).

Ryan, R. M. & Deci, E. L. (2001). On happiness and human

potentials: A review of research on hedonic and eudaimonic well-being. *Annual Review of Psychology, 52*(1), 141–66.

Schimpff, S. (2019). Loneliness is the New Smoking: How payers and providers should address it. *Managed Healthcare Executive.*

Shanafelt, T. D., Balch, C. M., Bechamps, G., Russell, T., Dyrbye, L., Satele, D., . . . & Freischlag, J. (2010). Burnout and medical errors among American surgeons. *Annals of Surgery, 251*(6), 995–1000.

Shenk, C. E., Putnam, F. W. & Noll, J. G. (2012). Experiential avoidance and the relationship between child maltreatment and PTSD symptoms: Preliminary evidence. *Child Abuse & Neglect, 36*(2), 118–26.

Tawfik, D. S., Profit, J., Morgenthaler, T. I., Satele, D. V., Sinsky, C. A., Dyrbye, L. N., . . . & Shanafelt, T. D. (2018). Physician burnout, well-being, and work unit safety grades in relationship to reported medical errors. *Mayo Clinic Proceedings, 93*(11), 1571–80. Elsevier.

Thompson, K. L., Hannan, S. M. & Miron, L. R. (2014). Fight, flight, and freeze: Threat sensitivity and emotion dysregulation in survivors of chronic childhood maltreatment. *Personality and Individual Differences, 69*, 28–32.

van der Kolk, B. A. (2014). *The Body Keeps the Score: Brain, mind, and body in the healing of trauma.* New York, NY: Viking Press.

Walker, P. (2013). *Complex PTSD: From surviving to thriving.* Azure Coyote.

Warren, B. (2012). *The Top Five Regrets of the Dying: A life transformed by the dearly departing* by Bronnie Ware. Proceedings (Baylor University Medical Center), *25*(3), 299–300

White, R. E. & Carlson, S. M. (2015). What would Batman do? Self-distancing improves executive function in young children. *Developmental Science, 19*(3), 419–26.

Xu, J. & Roberts, R. E. (2010). The power of positive emotions: It's a matter of life or death – Subjective well-being and longevity over 28 years in a general population. *Health Psychology, 29*(1), 9–19.

Resources

In the UK

If you are having a mental health crisis:
Call Samaritans 116-123 (completely free and confidential)
Website: www.samaritans.org.uk

To find a mental health professional in your area:
Check out https://www.bacp.co.uk/search/Therapists

For information on how to stop child abuse:
Contact NSPCC
Phone: 0800 1111 for Childline for children (24-hour helpline)
Or 0808 800 5000 for adults concerned about a child
(24-hour helpline)
Website: www.nspcc.org.uk

For reporting domestic violence:
Contact Refuge
Phone: 0808 2000 247 (24-hour helpline)
Website: www.refuge.org.uk

For survivors of sexual assault:

>To find your local services phone: 0808 802 9999
>
>>(daily, 12 to 2.30 p.m., 7 to 9.30 p.m.)
>
>Website: www.rapecrisis.org.uk
>
>Phone: 0808 168 9111 (24-hour helpline)
>
>Website: www.victimsupport.org

In the US

If you are having a mental health crisis:

>Call 1-800-273-8255 (available 24/7 free and confidential)
>
>Text: 'HOME' to 741-741 (available 24/7 free and confidential)

If you or a loved one experienced sexual assault:

>Call or message RAINN: 1(800) 656-4673 (available 24/7
>
>>free and confidential)
>
>Website: https://www.rainn.org

For reporting domestic violence:

>Call 1(800) 799-7233
>
>Website: https://www.thehotline.org

For information on how to stop child abuse:

>Call 1(800) 422-4453
>
>Website: https://www.childhelp.org/hotline/

To find a mental health professional in your area:

>Type in your zip code on https://www.psychologytoday.com

Acknowledgements

This work would not have been possible without the constant support of my incredible partner, Dustin. Thank you, honey, for all the hugs, for believing in me, and for bringing me coffee in the middle of the night in order to help me to keep writing. This book would also not be possible without my amazing editor, Andrew McAleer, whose guidance and faith in me has allowed me to keep writing throughout the years, thank you for believing in me. I would also like to thank my agent, Wendy Rohm, for her tireless work to support my writing, and Vince Alvendia, for his gorgeous artwork. I would like to express the deepest gratitude to the wonderful editors who worked on this book – Amanda Keats and Alison Tulett, thank you for all your wonderful feedback and support.

This book would also not be possible without the consultation and support from real-life superheroes: Liz, Erika, Alex, Adam, Chris, Saim, Ross, Lauren, and Denisse. Thank you for making the world a better place.

Finally, I would like to express my deepest gratitude to everyone who supported me through this process, especially my family – Dustin, Hunter, Eddie, Shaye, my mom, Sherry, Rich and Chase – and my incredible friends – Jenna, Jeff, Paxton, Sasha, Shawn, Phil, Eugene, Robin, Elina, Alan and Happy. Gary, thank you for supplying me with all the Bounty chocolate to help with my writing.

Thank you all for being wonderful.

Index

Note: page numbers in **bold** refer to diagrams.